D0760629

LET ME
EXPLAIN
BLACK
AGAIN

LET ME
EXPLAIN
BLACK
AGAIN

Exploring Blind Spots
and **Black Insights** for
Marketing & Understanding
**Black Culture and
Perspectives**

**PEPPER
MILLER**

Paramount Market Publishing, Inc.

Paramount Market Publishing, Inc.
274 North Goodman Street, STE D-214
Rochester, NY 14607
www.paramountbooks.com
607-275-8100

Publisher: James Madden
Editorial Director: Doris Walsh

Copyright © 2023 Pepper Miller

All rights reserved. No part of this book may be reproduced, stored in a retrieval system, or transmitted in any form or by any means, electronic, mechanical, photocopying, recording, or otherwise, without the prior written permission of the publisher. Further information may be obtained from Paramount Market Publishing, Inc., 274 North Goodman Street, STE D-214, Rochester, NY 14607.

This publication is designed to provide accurate and authoritative information in regard to the subject matter covered. It is sold with the understanding that the publisher is not engaged in rendering legal, accounting, or other professional services. If legal advice or other expert assistance is required, the services of a competent professional should be sought.

Cover photo: © 2021 Powell Creative Services

Library of Congress Catalog available
Cataloging in Publication Data available
ISBN 10: 1-941688-79-9
ISBN 13: 978-1-941688-79-3

Dedication

For Brandon, Devonna, and Jesse
You are our now and our future. I love you very much.

In Memory of ...

My parents

John Hunter—My Drew Bundini Brown—
My encouraging "corner man."

Ruth Hunter—For passing down an adventurous soul
and a spirit of curiosity.

My brother

Barney Hunter—A fearless warrior who left this world
too soon.

I miss you all. Thank you for leaving an indelible imprint
on my life that has contributed to who I am today.

Ken Smikle who brought the Black American marketing
community together via Target Market News Conferences
and Publications. The industry will never be the same.

Herb Kemp, my friend, mentor, and co-author of *What's
Black About It?* —I still miss you!

Arthur "Bud" McCullen: From 1995–2019, the best senior
analyst ever! We had a great run. RIP

Big Time Appreciation

Victoria Childress—My brilliant strategist, writer, creative, book contributor, and friend.

I am grateful for our special bond, me, the Boomer in the United States, and you, the Millennial in Orvieto, Italy, and the incredible journey during these 11+ years. And to think, as of this writing, we've never met in person! I could not have undertaken this journey without you.

Contents

Preface

What More Do You Want?
"You Finally Have a Black President. What More Do You Want?"

That's what a colleague asked me with a slight chuckle just before taking a sip of his cocktail. I'll call him Bob—a white male marketing executive. I didn't laugh with him but offered a somewhat unamused smile. Undoubtedly rhetorical, I wanted to answer Bob because these were the day-to-day questions I addressed with clients during office hours, in articles and in keynote speeches. But there we were, after hours, enjoying a cocktail reception hosted by a Chicago advertiser's society. It was a festive evening where we professionals let our hair down to mingle and put industry talk on DND until Monday morning. But that's just it. Industry talk for me is never finished because after twenty-five-plus years of doing this work, being Black in America is up for discussion twenty-four hours a day.

To answer Bob's question, "What more do I want?"—I want America to understand and celebrate Black value.

Let me explain . . .

President Barack Obama had taken office just a few months before the cocktail reception. I was thrilled to witness this incredible milestone in our country's history, as a Black American, and as a market researcher. I lead one of the few agencies in the country specializing in Black American market research, Hunter-Miller, Inc. I help decision-makers of large corporations understand the thoughts, behaviors, and motivating beliefs of Blacks in America. When I opened the doors of my Chicago-based agency in 1995, I hung my shingle to conduct research for the general market. But when I showed up to meetings as a brown-skinned Black woman, I was almost always told, "We will call you when we have something Black."

Back then, Black agencies like Burrell Communications, Proctor and Gardner, E. Morris Communications, The Chisholm-Mingo Group, and Black-owned companies like Soft Sheen and Luster Products provided opportunities for me to conduct research with Black consumers, and I loved it. Then and there, I found my calling: specializing in the African American consumer market. As the years went by, I found myself arguing about the need to separate what had become a hodgepodge of multi-cultural approaches as the industry's attempt in addressing multicultural consumers. I argued that valid, distinct segmenting and targeting was the best practice for Blacks, Latinos, Asians, Indigenous Peoples, and so forth. Research and advertising objectives would be well defined and I would conduct qualitative research with consumers to better understand who they are, what they believe and do and especially, why to all of the above. The result would be real people reading an ad, seeing a commercial or program, hearing something on the radio or attending an event that directly and deeply resonated with them. This would make them feel included and celebrated and positively influence consumer behavior. How does this happen? Research. Representation. Positive Realism. A genuine connection occurs when an individual within these minority groups encounters a touchpoint with a message that includes their language and echoes their beliefs and aspirations. Qualitative research delivers this type of impact; and it happens to be my specialty.

Nevertheless, research and advertising dollars have always been lean, when related to understanding America's multicultural population. It was obvious that targeting minorities was extrinsic. And perhaps it was enough to be thankful. *But I wanted more for us.*

Understanding the Black American Journey

The "What more do you want?" question from Bob was no surprise. These types of remarks are often expressed, in various forms, by people from the sales floor, to the boardroom conference table, and it's commonplace for me to address them head-on.

Black Americans have a long history of being neglected, as both marketplace consumers and workplace decision-makers, despite having compelling qualifications, influence, and spending power. I have conducted hundreds of research studies, spoken at large conferences and universities, consulted with nonprofit and private firms, and led workshops where my primary objective was to underscore Black value and why Black *still* matters in marketing.

During these events, I dive deep into the Black American journey, starting with the foundations of how our experience in America has shaped our present-day reality. I provide the framework for how we're different and why it has taken us so long to achieve a standard of living that more-privileged white Americans have enjoyed for generations.

I put the data and insights in context, illustrating how Blacks don't just show up with all their wonderment and complexities but must navigate systems designed to exclude them on a daily basis. I highlight what Black Americans value, how they want to be portrayed, and where the unconscious biases exist for decision makers who often determine how Black people are represented. My goal is to bring awareness where there is none; and, hopefully, help change perspectives.

Not Too Much to Ask

Blacks in America feel as if asking for fairness is asking for too much. It's audacious to want a win-win. You see, that's what *"What more do you want?"* really meant. Bob suggested that I should be happy with *some* victory and not much more than that. This line of thinking means it is unrealistic and unreasonable to expect both a win in the White House and a win in the business market. Yet since Obama's presidency, more lawmakers, state representatives, and senators of color are stepping into these influential seats of power in the government. I want to see these advancements echo across America in corporations and decision-making roles. Expecting a win-win is necessary, and it is entirely possible.

To be clear, this book isn't a political take on the ups and downs the research and advertising industry has experienced over the last two decades. It's not a political book at all. Instead, mentioning recent political administrations and events for this book is like a timestamp, serving as clues for where the country stands racially and societally.

Introduction

Why the Need to Explain Black Again

It is crucial not only to speak about Black Americans and their values in the most robust possible context but to ensure that those to whom I am speaking are leaning in and listening. Two key events demonstrate why now is the most opportune time for *Let Me Explain Black, Again.*

First, there is an opportunity to uncover the shift in the value of "Black" after the country's three catalytic disruptors: Trump, COVID, and George Floyd. There is more insight into understanding the language, beliefs, and behaviors of Black culture; how Black Americans are unapologetically different from mainstream; and what real inclusion and equality and celebration look like, why it still matters, and why it should not be feared by whites.

Second, there is an opportunity to learn about America's unbridled truth and specific "*aha!* moments" revealing America's blind spots—most often expressed using four little words: *"Pepper, I didn't know."*

We're in a time in our country's history where Black Americans are making an educational, economic, and social impact like never before, achieving record-breaking success, and advancing in their own right; however, they are not yet vested with the same liberties of white America. The Black Lives Matter and George Floyd protests have awakened many to Black America's plight, our value and contributions despite forced limitations, and, importantly, the fact that Blacks are *still* striving for equality and authentic inclusion.

Mellody Hobson, president of Ariel investments, eloquently expounds on the value of real inclusion. During a PwC Talks interview about her resounding TED Talk: *Being Color Brave,* Hobson challenges business leaders to confront racially exclusive practices, offering simple solutions when she said this:

> "When you (Black people) walk into a room, and there's no diversity, you immediately see it. A simple way of getting at diversity (is to ask the question), 'Is everyone in the room?' If you were trying to solve a really hard problem the best way to do it is with a group of diverse people including diverse intellect . . . invite people into your life that don't look like you, who don't think like you, and who don't come from where you come from."

When I started my journey of specializing in Black consumer market research and speaking to corporate America, most then were, and still are, white executives and decision-makers. Now I must admit, my delivery back then was rough. I accused, and I finger-pointed. My zeal was apparent, but not in a way that contributed to change.

As I improved my approach, I understood that I needed to meet clients where they were, on a human level. When I did this, the art of conversation and its effectiveness became apparent. I began considering my insights and presentations as an opportunity for activism and diplomacy. Over time, I reframed the story, improved my delivery, and showed up instead with thought-leading, award-winning dialogue.

When I explain Black, I am not casting a punitive shadow over white America. Think of this book as a resource tool with insights, stats, quotes, and stories to support the rationale for understanding "the why" about Black America and investing in this distinctive and desirable segment. Also, it's essential to think of this book as a proverbial table. I'm pulling up my chair to start the conversation about Black in a way that underscores the importance of Black influence and value, as well as looking at the full, unbridled truth about Black American history, how Black people are different and why these differences need to be embraced by all. I'm inviting you to pull up your chair, be "color brave," and learn how authentic connection leads to loyalty.

How to Use this Book

I wrote *What's Black About It* (with the late Herbert Kemp, Jr.) and *Black STILL Matters in Marketing* in 2005 and 2012, respectively.

Those books were written to provide rarely discussed insights and research-backed data on the spending power, influence and value of Black American consumers. Lately, my presentations and keynotes echo what this book will cover: Black America in context, the fundamentals of Black identity, how different treatment has influenced different behavior, how Black youth are not as mainstream as some may think, and a timeline that depicts Black America's awakenings toward equality—which has been the most important achievement for Blacks. I delve into the back-stories to help marketers and decision-makers fully understand the breadth and depth of deeply rooted beliefs that influence attitudes that lead to particular perspectives and behaviors—starting with the Black lens.

Use this book:

As a resource and guidebook for centering and making a case for Black consumer value.

For a deep dive into the fundamentals of Black history, identity, language, beliefs, and behaviors.

To grab the most current stats on Black men, women, immigrants, LGBTQ+ and youth.

To discover the link between blind spots and unconscious biases that affect everyday decision making as a resource for identifying popular Black community spaces.

To explore my unique observations and insights on the market's go-to segment in Black Millennial and Gen Z consumers.

To understand the intricacies and importance of Black community and relationships.

For a crash course on what it takes to be a winning brand that Black consumers seek.

Use this book, and the stories and statistics within, to have more meaningful conversations. We need more talkers *and* more listeners. We need more dialogue from various perspectives in this country—at home, in boardrooms and classrooms, in religious institutions, and across the aisles of politics, race, and gender. Society and corporate America are making the same outdated observations and asking the same outdated questions about what they know and what they think about when it comes to Black people. Unfortunately, though, many of their perceptions are false. This book will set you on the right path to identify blind spots and seize opportunities that can establish a lasting connection and meaningful engagement.

Let Me Explain Black, Again is a guide for leaders, decision-makers, and consumers. Key chapters include an insight or opportunity statement to help answer the "So what, now what?" questions. You can also use the insights to springboard your research to ultimately garner a better understanding of and connection with Black America. I hope the stories and methods presented here will help everyone close the cultural awareness gap and change "I didn't know" to "I know, celebrate, and value Black consumers."

✖

What Does It Mean?

Insights, Observations, and Cultural Nuances

An **insight** is the comprehending of a person or thing's true nature, especially through intuitive understanding. It is also a presentation of the motivational forces behind a person's actions, thoughts or behavior.

The information presented in this book is a collection of insights I've gathered over the years that examine Black people, their history, beliefs, behaviors, and buying habits.

Observations are simply raw data points of information, without context that gives them meaning.

In this book, I share observations that have a profound place in today's discussion about race, equality, and value in the marketplace. Throughout this book I have been careful to point out stories or instances that are observations, and information that is researched and sourced.

Cultural nuances are subtle differences in meaning or expressions that are oftentimes unwritten, unspoken rules of understanding relative to a particular race or culture. These nuances are important for communicating effectively and avoiding miscommunications.

An example of a cultural nuance would be flipping the script on Black stereotypes—showing Black men as involved caretakers, e.g., taking care of a baby, a child, or a number of children; divorced parents positively co-parenting their children etc.

PART ONE

America's Abiding Blind Spot is Black

Exploring Unconscious Biases and Their Origins

I Didn't Know

I wrote my last book in 2012. The first two, *What's Black About It?* and *Black STILL Matters in Marketing,* explained Black consumers quite thoroughly. But I decided to write *Let Me Explain Black, Again* because four repetitive but important words have been the single most echoed comment I've heard during these last ten years: *"Pepper, I didn't know."*

After I wrap a research study, speaking engagement, or my flagship Black Insights workshops and presentations, without fail, *someone* from the audience comes up to me confidentially to say, "Pepper, I didn't know."

What Don't They Know?

Most people, especially corporate decision-makers, have not made the connection between Black consumer behavior and Black American history. I simply tell the American story from the Black perspective, and it has proved to be the transformative ingredient that helps business leaders understand "the why." The total depth of American history that provides marketing and engagement insight is critical to understanding Black American behavior. Before they leave, they let me know that something in my speech helped them see how Black consumers are valuable, unique or different from any other group of people in the United States.

American-born Black people whose ancestors were enslaved people or descendants of enslaved people especially have a different perspective on nearly everything that affects their daily lives. Their history is different from other Black people in America and other minorities. This difference in history begets a different lens—a different way of looking at the country they call home and the people they call fellow citizens.

Exploring this perspective, this Black lens, is critical to understanding how they see themselves and how others see them. Years of egregious treatment, ongoing discrimination, biases, and microaggressions in every American institute have resulted in beliefs and behaviors that, if simply observed but not put into context, prompt some to judge Black people unfairly.

Some executives are now pondering this chasm of knowledge. They are wondering what happened. As they begin an introspective examination of their beliefs and behavior, three key areas emerge as catalysts for their "I didn't know" *aha!* moments:

1. Certainty of a post-racial mindset

2. Not seeing racism as a problem

3. The three catalytic disrupters:
   Trump/COVID/Murder of George Floyd

Let me explain each . . .

1. We're <u>not</u> living in a post-racial society? *I didn't know!*

A Black president, Black celebrities and Black socio-economic progress leads America to think we're post racial.

In 2008, when the people of the United States elected their first Black president, "Finally," I thought, "We're going to see some real changes around here." A Black man in office certainly gave many of us that impression. I gleefully predicted that more attention and resources in market research, media, and advertising would be provided for minority markets.

I imagined seeing racially diverse commercials reflecting the actual makeup of America, with visuals and messaging representing the whole. I thought that surely if President Obama could win the Oval Office, more Black men and women would be recognized as leaders in their respective positions across the country. I fully embraced this surreal feeling of living, working and thriving in the direction of a post-racial America. For once, I let my mind soar to all the wonderful possibilities of what America could be. Black people could finally achieve equality after generations of being in the shadows. And in the industry, I expected investments to increase for Black consumer marketing. It would mean a boom in business, especially since Black agencies and media have been endangered for decades.

I soon discovered that my predictions were way too ambitious. My glee was premature. None of that happened. In fact, the opposite happened. Racial division and tension began to overhaul what progress we as a country had supposedly already made. The country was divided: those who disapproved of such 'change' and those who celebrated it.

Leaders utter the words "I didn't know" because the industry's rationale was this: *"They have a Black president. There are countless Black athletes, entertainers and public-figure millionaires. Why is it necessary to focus on Black Americans—they speak English, don't they? What about other minorities?"* This post-racial agenda influenced business leaders to divest and instead promote a post-racial mindset in the market. The result was a complete loss of interest in Black Americans as consumers worth targeting. I called it *The Great Black Advertising, Marketing, Media and Market Research Regression*.

Multicultural departments were dismantled, and opportunities in consumer packaged goods and independent research think tanks were canceled. There were immediate budget cuts in Black and multicultural consumer research and advertising. A large percentage of business for ethnic agencies was redirected to general market agencies. Categorically, the multicultural market dissolved into Total Market.[1] Black media and advertising and research firms were no longer relevant, including mine. The gross absence of minority interest made those streamlined multicultural attempts that I complained about in previous years seem like glory days. It was indeed a confusing time.

What was happening in the country and the industry after the election of the nation's first Black president, and to us, was a stark contrast to how we imagined our nation's future. We thought, naively perhaps, that the election of President Obama would usher in an awakening. We thought there was a shift on the horizon towards equality because, after all, Black people didn't elect President Obama on their own. The 2008 election resulted in people from all backgrounds coming together to appoint a man they believed could move the country forward. For Black America, this was a sign that America as a whole was finally ready to embrace Black like it had never been able to do in its young, marred history.

2. I didn't know racism was still a problem in America.

Under the Trump administration which began in 2017, the division among Americans widened even more as many Trump supporters welcomed his divisive tactics. For example, his comments and tweets ranged from anti-immigrant sentiments to negative comments about the Latino community when he described them as "criminals" and "rapists." He referred to Haiti and African countries as "shit holes," described Baltimore's low-income Black community as a "rat and rodent-infested mess," and labeled COVID-19 as the "Chinese virus." It didn't stop with his words. He gave the nod for agencies to separate and cage Latino refugee families. His rhetoric and decisions broadened the existing racial division, causing tension between several white conservative groups and Black, Latino, and Asian American citizens.

This was America's first modern-age eye-opening, *aha!* moment. The sharp contrast between realizing America's racial divide in 2016 and thinking America was post-racial just a few years prior is one reason why executives confess, "I didn't know."

After the Civil Rights Movement, high-earning, educated Black Americans who participate in lifestyles that mirror the mainstream experience began to rise. Today in addition to everyday people, public figures like Oprah, Beyoncé, the Obamas, LeBron James, other high-profile professionals, and other high-income earners are often perceived by business leaders and society as representing the end of Black Americans' struggle for equality. They think *"It's a thing of the past."* Despite social and economic progress, they often fail to see how the Black American experience is still more challenging than the white American experience.

We are not post-racial in America. Our country still has a debilitating problem with race and it won't go away simply because a percentage of the Black population is considered to be rich.

Conversations, like the ones I have with clients on a daily basis, are a start to figuring out how to get closer to a post-racial society. I'm aware, though, that these types of conversations take bold talkers *and* bold listeners. In this new era of when people are easily offended, it is tricky to proclaim a stance or state a personal opinion on race related matters. Some believe discussing race and differences, in any capacity is divisive, when that couldn't be further from the truth. *Not* talking about race, culture and the things that make us different *is* divisive. Refusing to acknowledge Black people for who they are, deprives them of their identity. At the same time white privilege is a touchy subject, too; and while it is uncomfortable, it's necessary to discuss. Black American history exists. White privilege exists. And all of it influences what America sees and doesn't see.

It is crucial for non-Black readers to know that when I write about my experiences and when I assess various situations as examples and data points, my use of the terms, racism, racist, prejudice and bias is intended to call a thing a thing and to ultimately serve as a learning opportunity.

3. Three catalytic disruptors led to America's overdue awakening

My good friend, George Fraser, a serial entrepreneur, master networker, author, and CEO of FrasNet, Inc., said this about these three disruptors:

> "Marketing (and life as we know it) will forever be defined as pre- and post-Trump, COVID, and George Floyd."

Fraser is right.

In the initial wave of the global pandemic that hit the United States particularly hard, during the months following George Floyd's murder and again near the end of Trump's presidency, my phone wouldn't stop ringing and my inbox was full. Businesses and brands needed help. There was a nation of mixed emotions, expressions and reactions and many leaders were bewildered on how to best connect themselves and their brand to Black America.

I began to present a compelling case for Black value, offering research and insights specifically related to these three disruptors in my Black Insights presentations, and after hearing the information, most of these leaders would lean in and listen with amazement, ask follow-up questions and want to share the findings with their teams. It gave them pause. It was likely the first time they heard events and situations that contradicted their beliefs about America.

That point in time on a corporate and societal level, was a big moment in America, but surprisingly enough, it was not big enough to make significant change. Soon after, it was back to business as usual. Nevertheless, a seed had been planted.

The combination of Trump's leadership and excessive violence against Black people created the perfect storm that caused America to have an "overdue awakening," as coined by *Time* magazine.

Remember Ahmaud Arbery, murdered while jogging by three white men; Breonna Taylor, killed in her home during an early morning raid by police who had incorrect information; the viral video of an agitated white lady, Amy Cooper, calling and falsely reporting to the police that a birdwatcher, Chris Cooper, a Black man had attacked her; and the heinous murder of George Floyd by a police officer.

Collectively, these events shed an embarrassing light on America. Black America has long known and lived these horrors, but it was not broadcast on the world's stage until 2020: Black America continues to live and die at the hands of systemic racism, while white America turns a blind eye.

In the years that I listened to embarrassed and humble business leaders confess "*I didn't know,*" I suspect their "*I didn't know*" really meant that they didn't realize their complicity, not in being racists per se, but in racism's close relatives: privilege and microaggression. I think many walk away, realizing there's something about themselves they've not acknowledged, mainly how privilege plays a prominent role in their lives.

After sharing the Black insights as a guest on *The Happy Market Research Podcast*, host Jamin Brazil said this:

> "[I'm on a quest to] uncover the role diversity plays in the research we do daily. As a white guy, I didn't think that I was tainted by racism or prejudice. I was blown away by my own embedded prejudices that I simply was not aware of. I had been unknowingly conditioned to have these prejudices."

In a challenge to his listeners, he continued . . . "I hope you'd be willing to challenge yourself . . . and double-triple-check your own biases. Ask yourself, how can I build a more inclusive team at the company I work at right now?"

Moving beyond "I Didn't Know"

My track record as a thought-leader, and one who consistently works with big brands like AARP, BRAVO, CNN, McDonald's, Procter & Gamble, Unilever, Walgreens, The Chicago Symphony Orchestra, and many more, has helped business leaders, who thought they knew Black consumers, understand them on a deeper level.

We won't get anywhere if our first reaction to uncomfortable conversations is to be defensive. In order to approach any part of the tangled web of race and inequality in market research, marketing and advertising, it is imperative to grasp some fundamentals of the Black psyche. Without getting into technical psychology, getting to the "why" responsible for Black beliefs and behaviors will help uncover areas where there are preconceptions—opening your eyes to a wider scope of who we're talking about when we talk about Black lives and Black value.

Consider our country's history. Consider that to be Black was, not that long ago, an identity wrought with servitude of being less than a human being. With that consideration, when Black people say "Black lives matter," consider who is speaking and why they need to proclaim a statement like that. Also, if you will, consider that a response "white lives matter, too" is a defensive response. Let's look at the "why" before we look to overshadow the other, in order to defend or protect yourself.

To discover these uncomfortable truths allows us to examine how we got here. To change our future and improve how society and brands connect to Black culture in a meaningful way requires an honest look at how unconscious bias and ill-informed decisions have created and perpetuated the disconnect.

Note

1. *Total Market strategy* is defined by the Association of Hispanic Advertising Agencies as a marketing approach followed by corporations with their trusted internal and external partners which proactively integrates diverse segment considerations. This is done from inception, through the entire strategic process and execution with the goal of enhancing value and growth effectiveness In marketing communications, this could lead to either one fully integrated cross cultural approach, individual approaches, or both in many cases, but always aligned under one strategy."
   Source: "The Promise and Reality of 'Total Market' and How CMOs Need to Address It," Pepper Miller, forbes.com, 8/23/2016

The Dangers of Blind Spots

The Blind Spot Test

A blind spot is a void or block in a person's line of sight—an absence of information so small that the brain works to fill in peripheral details in the void of that space, rendering the person oblivious *or blind* to the fact that a void even exists, or that something was ever missing. A blind spot is rarely obvious from a personal perspective, but often obvious to others. Everyone has blind spots; let's test that theory.

A useful test of our physical inability to see everything all at once is The Blind Spot Test. It's used by optometrists and pathologists in varying degrees to determine just how clear or obstructed one's vision might be. Below, there is a black "dot" on the left and a black "X" on the right. First, completely cover or close your right eye. Next, focus your left eye on the "X." Slowly bring this book or screen closer to your face—don't lose focus of the "X." At a particular point, the black "dot" on the left will disappear. *That* is your blind spot.

● ✖

Notice that you didn't observe a void where the black dot is. Your brain simply filled in that blind spot space with more white space. What just happened isn't an optical illusion. It's a flaw in our anatomical makeup. It is our human inability to see everything all at once.

It happens when we enter an empty room or a crowded one. It happens on the road, in the car. What is the importance of discovering our blind spots? Not seeing can be dangerous! Not only are blind spots a physical reality, but a psycho-emotional one as well. In our personal and professional lives, blind spots exist and that influences our beliefs and behaviors.

The dangers of blind spots are situated just there in that obscure, subliminal, and unconscious space of our vision, mind, and perspectives.

What's interesting is that no one person can positively identify the blind spots of another. Sure, I can form an opinion based on certain signs about whether a friend or colleague may have a blind spot or two. As well as for myself: I can constructively take the feedback and cues from friends or colleagues who tell me, "Pepper, you're not getting it!" Only then might I begin to question my own clarity—**because not only do we all think we can see everything clearly, all the time, we all think we're right.** Without some indication that I'm missing the point of a friend's argument, sharing an insensitive response to a dialogue, or just not seeing the big deal with something I said, how would I ever know?

When I think about the term "blind spot," I automatically think about blind spots on the road while driving. In this instance, blind spots are caused by something obstructing my view—likely a panel in the car that blocks my full range of sight or a rear view mirror that cannot show me the full range and periphery of my immediate area.

When I was a young girl, riding sometimes in the backseat of my parents' car or, on lucky days, the front seat, I took notice of all the little gestures they made while driving. For kids, seeing your parents operate this big fancy machinery that transports you to magical, and sometimes mundane, places is thrilling. Driving is one of those things that makes a kid want to be a grown-up. After my mother drove the car, my father sometimes needed to adjust the seat position or the steering wheel, but positioning the mirrors seemed especially important. On those winter Chicago mornings, my father would clear the snow from the front and back windows and the side mirrors. My mother would start the engine to warm the car. All of those little gestures made sense to me. But some things they did, didn't make sense. I learned that the little stick on the side of the steering wheel was to signal that they were turning a corner or changing lanes. I learned how to turn on the headlights and windshield wipers. From where I sat in the passenger seat, short and very much a novice, the purview of my passenger mirror only showed me an up-close view of the car door. I thought they were looking at the car door the whole time . . . but why? I later learned, sitting on my dad's lap in the driver's seat, that from his vantage point, that passenger mirror allowed him to see things behind and to the right of the car. As I got older and started practicing driving myself, I understood that the passenger mirror was helpful, but it wasn't enough.

I remember thinking this particular gesture they did while driving was silly. They would look over to check the mirror, look out the window, turn their head, look out the window again, and check the mirror again, all in a matter of seconds, before reversing the car out of the driveway or changing lanes on the highway. Why couldn't they just use the mirrors to see? Why all this head-turning, checking, looking out, looking over and checking, again—over and over? Was all that necessary?

Yes. I eventually understood that *not* diligently turning and checking and looking at every possible angle is a dangerous choice. The dangers of blind spots are the most severe and fatal when I neglect my duty to check—because it could lead to something being irreparably damaged or someone being hurt or worse. As a responsible driver, it is my job to make sure I check—to be sure I know. If I fail to check, I cannot absolve myself of fault by saying, "I didn't know." It is my job and my duty *to know.*

Being in the driver's seat, that is, being a leader in my own respect, I now understand that the mirrors inside and outside my car don't show the entire picture of the world around me. I read somewhere once that the fact that blind spots exist reminds me that mirrors should never be a substitute for first-hand judgment. For our discussion in this book, the mirror in this analogy is your consciousness. Have you ever used your knowledge, something you know to be true, to dismiss new information or ignore a gut feeling? Doing this is the same process the brain is subjected to when encountering a blind spot. It fills in the missing pieces with peripheral information. That is, we often prefer what we think we know, over something new or different, that could be the truth. It is sometimes easier to continue to believe false or outdated information even in the presence of new, fact-based information.

Let's put this in context. Generalizations are a type of blind spot and I want to contextualize how generalizations and stereotypes create blind spots that negatively affect Black consumers. History has shown how campaigns that portrayed Black people in a certain negative light, permeated America, especially the south. These campaigns showed Black men as animalistic and dangerous, and Black women as servants. It showed Black people habitually eating certain types of food and dressing a certain type of way. When a marketer or campaign lead decides to cast a Black kid in an ad and clothe him in a sweatshirt with the message "Coolest Monkey in the Jungle" or show a popular R&B vocalist singing about fried chicken and dancing on the counter of a fast food restaurant, because all Black people are like this—*that* is a blind spot!

Blind spots, in this book, are unconscious biases. I use these terms interchangeably to describe the void or block in a person's perspective and the absence or denial of information that renders a person oblivious, *or blind,* to the fact that their beliefs and behaviors are shaped by realities they can't see.

What Are Your Blind Spots?

What are the unconscious biases you can't or refuse to see? How might you generalize or stereotype Black people, consciously or subconsciously refusing to create a more complete, and accurate picture about who they are?

My hope and the best outcome would be that you have clarity and an *aha!* moment of your own that will encourage you to see Black people and Black consumers as valuable, on a deeper, more insightful level.

In the following chapters, we're going to explore the missing peripheral data, and replace it with Black insights that paint the most accurate picture of who Black American consumers are today. We're going to explore the seven most common blind spots or unconscious biases in our industry, and I believe that the research I've put into the stories and the Black insights you will discover throughout this book will give leaders and consumers a complete picture.

The tools in this book can help leaders improve their brand engagement, create better campaigns, and connect with Black Americans.

It's time to do a Blind Spot Test check for yourself, except this time, it's not looking at a black "dot" and an "X." Instead, you will focus on your own thoughts and habits, especially the areas where you're absolutely sure you're doing it right. Question those aspects of yourself. Inquire with others to examine the areas you just can't see yourself. *And be honest.*

It is my hope that you make some self-discoveries. Don't be afraid to question and challenge your own biases. Only then can you do the necessary work to see, with better clarity, the people and their world around you.

PART TWO

Seven Top Leadership Blind Spots

Unpacking Unconscious Biases

Racially speaking, Americans are often focused on the blown-out, overt, macro version of racism—and it is still a challenge America faces. Today, the inequality that is found in the marketing and market research industries, and throughout many of America's systems, stems from something more subtle.

Many of you have probably heard the term *micro-aggressions,* but have you heard of micro-biases and micro-inequities? These terms focus on specific types of microaggressions, calling attention to the behaviors and beliefs of those who benefit from privilege. You must be willing to ask yourself what beliefs you hold about yourself or Black people that might unintentionally yet directly influence the comments you make, the jokes you tell and the decisions that govern the lives and well-being of those who live and work alongside you every day. Biases fuel exclusion. Biases justify inequality. These covert unconscious beliefs and behaviors make inclusivity in market research difficult to achieve.

> **Microaggression**
> A statement, action, or incident regarded as an instance of indirect, subtle, or unintentional discrimination against members of a marginalized group such as a racial or ethnic minority.
> —*Google Oxford Dictionary*

Misrepresentation, misappropriation, the perpetuation of stereotypes, homogenization and erasure of cultural history and present-day prejudices all stem, not just from acts of overt and covert racism. They come from these explicit and implicit micro-biases and micro-inequities, of which business leaders and society may not even be fully aware. When those who are aware try to call attention to actions that aren't fatal or necessarily life-threatening, but *are* harmful to their well-being, they're often met with denial and repudiation.

If I performed The Blind Spot Test with a friend, but never explained the rules and that friend never saw the black "dot," that friend might fervently believe that the black dot was never there. I know it's there. But my friend is blind to it.

When one's knee-jerk reaction is to deny the existence of bias, there's always a chance one could be wrong. Silence and the refusal to examine oneself to investigate one's intentions and errors stifle any possible progress and solutions. In order to achieve true equality in market research and advertising practices, everyone must be willing to listen to what Black people are trying to convey about being included and equal.

Unconscious Bias Is Still Bias.

Delving into the world of Black culture (and other minority cultures) for a white researcher or marketer might seem daunting. It could also seem inconsequential if the preconception or generalization is that no real insights will result from the research or study. We'll delve into the intricacies of representation in the market research industry in Chapter 21; however, it should be a given that researchers must approach research spaces without bias. They *should,* but I know bias happens all too often.

When examining your own biases, I caution you not to take the path of least resistance. Do the work now to understand, for the long term, who these valuable targets are. Not only will you discover their history but also how resilient, open-minded and optimistic Black people are as a people.

It's possible to learn about and engage with people for whom you think no commonalities exist. You may discover there are numerous qualities that improve your life and your work.

There are all types of stigmas placed on people who are different from the mainstream majority, and it's often concluded that they're somehow deficient, broken, unable to keep up or perform as the majority does because of those differences. What if you discover those stigmas simply are not true?

America has a history of homogenizing the non-white cultural experience. One way to embrace being "color brave" is to use these differences as opportunities for dialogue and appreciation. There are centuries of misinformation that have prevented society from seeing the realities of Black life. These blind spots are the root of America's misconceptions and the basis of why so many lead with fear, hate and ignorance about Black people in America. Let's delve into the seven most common blind spots that I've observed as a researcher in America.

3

Blind Spot #1

The Avoidance of America's Unbridled History

Different History, Different Treatment, Different Beliefs and Behaviors that Define Black America

The most basic and fundamental piece of knowledge upon which to build your understanding of Black, is that Black history is not the same as white history. Blacks have an entirely different historical experience in this country; they are treated differently and this collective experience besets their beliefs and behavior. Let me explain . . .

First: What the Black Lens Is

The Black Lens is the foundation and perspective by which Black people see themselves and how they perceive how others see them. It is a perspective hardwired by personal experiences and the experiences of their family and ancestors. In order to "get Black," you must set your personal perspectives aside and look through this lens. Black beliefs and behaviors are the subjects of interest for market researchers, but exploring beliefs and behaviors based on such a complex history is not so simple. If you find yourself wondering . . .

Why are they like that?

Why can't they move past that dark period of American history?

Why don't they pull themselves up by their bootstraps and achieve something? After all, this is America!

. . . you would benefit by leading with empathy and approaching those questions through the framing of the Black lens. The only way one could ask these types of questions is not fully understanding the impact of America's historical events on Black America.

I share, during my Black Insights presentations, that we didn't just show up with all of our wonderment and complexities. There is a reason why Blacks are behind and have a distrust towards American systems and institutions. Consider that 250 years of slavery, 88 years of Jim Crow, 65 years of separate but equal, 35 years of housing discrimination and redlining and centuries of legislation that prevents Black people from having the same opportunities as white people and how this treatment has impacted the Black community and impeded Black progress.[1]

Ta-Nehisi Coates' summary of the Black American experience above chronicles centuries of egregious treatment of Black people in contrast to any other race in the United States.

While living in the segregated south for five years as a young child, I never thought about being Black, or different, or whites seeing me as less than, until I witnessed how it was perfectly legal to stifle some freedoms and segregate Black Americans' experiences. This wasn't centuries ago, but within my lifetime and the lifetimes of millions. What's more, is that I've observed reports that those discriminations, while now illegal, continue to happen in various ways that are covert enough to be difficult to prove.

This historical lens is the most important insight for business leaders and brands to understand. It is critical for strategy creation, creative development, media planning and market research. It provides the foundational connection for understanding Black America and especially U.S.-born Blacks. Every cultural belief, every cultural behavior ladders back to this lens. Ignoring this lens has resulted in missteps and missed opportunities.

When developing a strategic platform for this audience (or mainstream audiences) business leaders should always ask their teams, *"What are the Black insights?"* It's a powerful question to ask, because being observant of this lens, and the undeniable Black influence, provides the opportunity to get it right with Black America and mainstream.

Second: Different Treatment

If there were ever a benefit to living under segregation laws, it would be that Black people were forced to live amongst one another exclusively, and that brought about partnerships and camaraderie that benefited everyone within that community.

The story that follows is an historical recounting, that sheds light on the power of community, and the price Black people paid, for daring to be equal.

Remembering What Happened to the Prosperous Black Wall Street

Welcome to the bustling Greenwood sector of Tulsa, Oklahoma, a beacon of Black wealth in a 40-block community, center-lined with shops, cafes, nightclubs, parks, theaters, doctor's offices, hotels and restaurants, auto repair shops, and pool halls—you name it, they had it. It was a "made by us, for us, owned and operated by us" type of community; a proud sight indeed. Surrounding their little city within a city, was their residential community of lovely, picturesque one- and two-story homes, cab companies and rooming houses. They lived, worked, played, went to school and enjoyed American life in this haven, so much so that it was dubbed the 'Black Wall Street.' Everyone was safe. Everyone was thriving.

There was a boy, little Johnny Rowland, a teenage shoe shiner who liked to be called "Diamond Dick." He always showed up well-dressed, presentable and confident. He wore diamond rings on every finger and loved the finer things. His extravagant personality and hard-working mentality made him popular and well-liked by his frequent downtown patrons. In fact, he enjoyed a comfortable, vibrant life shining shoes, so much so that he stopped showing up for class at the all-Black segregated Booker T. Washington High School in Greenwood.

He was a typical kid, like many Black teenage boys in this day, who experienced a renaissance in civil, social, and economic American life for

Black folks following the Emancipation Proclamation of 1863, signed into law fifty-eight years earlier. The generation of his grandparents fought in the Civil War that ended slavery, and his parents' generation were born during and just after Reconstruction.

They fought overseas in the first World War. When life outside the plantation and integration into society proved iniquitous and even dangerous, his grandparents were the ones who decided to take liberty and happiness into their own hands, building their own communities and encouraging their children to fight for their country.

They're the ones whose great-greats lost $57 million in 1874, along with other newly emancipated slaves and Black soldiers who fought in the Civil War. Their savings were embezzled by white banking overseers, causing the collapse of The Freedmen's Bank and Trust Company. But they persevered. These two preceding generations were driven by determination. Their pride in recovering, remaining a strong people, creating a better life, and defending their country is the source of his pride and confidence. He inherited progress. And that was something. But he should have inherited wealth and land. Yet the resounding, resilient spirit of his community shows just how capable, intelligent, and progressive Black Americans are and it shows up in his work and his way of being. He's got good paternal figures to look up to, good maternal support, soul-feeding cuisine, arts, music and entertainment, healthcare, and just about everything he needed at his doorstep, including an opportunity to make money and make a name for himself in Greenwood.

Imaginably, the white people of Tulsa weren't thrilled with this so-called "Black Wall Street" and Greenwood's success. Rumors of the Harlem Renaissance (then called the New Negro Movement) seemed to reverberate to nearly every corner of the nation where progressive Black people lived and worked. Considering the social and economic damages that most Americans were enduring after World War I, life in America was bewildering for many. This generation would later be named "The Lost Generation" as much of their identity that was formed prior to the war, such as their way of life in the confederate Jim Crow South and the way of life in the North, was lost, leaving them directionless. Factory jobs and opportunities that were blocked and Black Codes that restricted African Americans' economic activity and free movement were slowly being lifted.

In the years prior to 1921, a series of attacks on these progressive Black communities throughout the country spurred what was known as the Red Summer.[2] Again and again, in Rosewood, Ocoee, Chicago, Elaine, and other cities nationwide, there would be a single event of a perceived crime, allegedly perpetrated by a Black man, uninvestigated, and often instigated by front-page newspaper headlines, that would incite race riots led by angry white mobs. Massacres and lynchings of Black people prevailed throughout the country, most often with the inciters unprosecuted.

But these alleged crimes weren't the culprit of entire communities being raided and burned; people being killed or displaced. Economic empowerment, equity, and equality was. So it was known throughout Black communities everywhere to tread carefully, especially if you were a Black man.

It was Memorial Day week of 1921, the much-anticipated kick-off for the summer, when "Diamond Dick" Rowland fatefully tripped into a young white girl, Sarah Paige. She was operating the elevator where Rowland was, and her scream, heard by a nearby clerk, set off a chain of events that would end it all for the hard-working Americans in Greenwood.

The Tulsa Tribune, Tulsa's local newspaper, falsely reported that a Black man assaulted a white teenage girl, and an angry mob quickly formed outside of the jailhouse in downtown Tulsa. The police had previously found and arrested Diamond Dick Rowland, providing the newspaper with these shallow details of the young man's name and description, but not much more than that—no warning of pending investigation and no indication that the boy was innocent. In fact, that article very much insinuated his guilt. Rowland's Greenwood community, having witnessed his arrest, hearing rumors of a lynching, and knowing all too well how these types of things play out, hurried down-town, too. These were his family's friends, community business owners, and neighbors—former World War vets, armed and prepared to defend their young son. Expectedly, the scene at the jailhouse was chaotic. Greenwood's fears were confirmed. The people of Tulsa wanted swift justice and there was no middle ground. A brawl turned into a deadly shoot-out between the two groups.

It wasn't just Rowland's perceived transgression. It was the Black people as a whole. To many Black Tulsans, something had to be done.

Hours after the fatal brawl in downtown Tulsa, hordes of white men descended upon the forty-five blocks of Greenwood with guns, shotguns, rifles, and firebombs. They fired upon any person of color in sight. They shot out the windows to *The Tulsa Star*, The Dreamland Theater, Little Rose Beauty Salon, and Bell & Little Cafe. As most women and children took refuge in their homes, their men tried to form a small legion against the attackers. They were outnumbered.

For what seemed like days of terror, the next dozen hours would completely level what was known as Greenwood. Not a single business was left standing. More than 300 Blacks—men, women, and children were murdered. Businesses were looted, firebombed, and burned to the ground. Forty square blocks of over twelve hundred African American homes, including hospitals, schools, churches, and 150 businesses, were destroyed. Nine thousand Black Americans were left homeless and lived in tents well into the winter of 1921.[3]

Only hours after that, planes flew overhead and sprayed turpentine and nitroglycerin bombs throughout the business and residential parts of Greenwood. And the remaining Greenwood residents had nowhere to go.

The story of Greenwood, Oklahoma, was all but forgotten as part of American History until just a few short years ago—even within the Black community. From generation to generation, there are many passed-down stories of pride and despair, written and verbal. But some stories were just too difficult to utter. Forgetting those traumas allowed

Black people during that time to simply survive another day. But they never really did forget. Many Black Americans simply exist and survive with these generational traumas—most unaware how their lineage's history affects their everyday lives.

When business leaders and others ask, "What's wrong with them?" . . . here's something to ponder:

Black America Is Behind Because They Are *Supposed* to Be Behind.

Where would Black America be today had Black Wall Street survived? Where would Black Americans be today if the money saved in the Freedman's Bank, by former slaves and Black soldiers who fought in the Civil War, had not been stolen?

FOLO: The Fear of Losing Out

CEO and senior strategist Ivan Burwell, founder of Street Source Marketing, partnered with me to write about the Fear of Losing Out (FOLO) for medium.com. In our article "The FOLO Syndrome and Why Marketers are Running Scared," we ask:

> "Why do certain people believe others have to lose in order for themselves to gain? Why can't there be a coexistence of all of us winning while maintaining alignment within our world?"

FOLO is the belief that one has to take something and claim it as their discovery or the belief that, for our kind to thrive, the "other" must suffer.

Flamboyant fashion maven, actor, and activist Billy Porter attempts to ease this popular FOLO belief as explained during an interview with *Essence* magazine:

> ". . . we don't want vengeance . . . We want our rights. We want equality. We want to be treated like human beings. We want to know that we can walk out of our houses and not be under threat of death every single day simply because of the color of our skin."

For many white Americans, the election of Barack Obama as the first Black president should have eased or forgiven past injustices, and it also should have elevated Black America to a place of equality. In contrast, a 2019 Pew Research Study on Social Trends revealed that Blacks are more likely than whites to believe that equality is out of their reach; 50 percent vs. 7 percent, respectively.

Many mainstream Americans are reluctant to change their mindset and thinking from an option to choose not to see, acknowledge, and care about America's history and those it affected. At a certain point, one must take the step to choose the truth and what your role will be in achieving a truly post-racial America.

Third: Different Beliefs and Behaviors

Due to Black Americans' different history and treatment, they have different beliefs and behaviors, many of which ladder back to the Black historical lens. These characteristics, often unknowing, under the radar, and ignored by marketers, are essential for understanding and engaging Black Americans. They can lead brands to broader insights, add value to a brand, and a competitive edge for strategies, creative briefs, marketing, media plans, etc. Let me explain with a few examples . . .

Respect Is King

Every person wants to be respected, and given the history of Black Americans, respect tends to be highly important. To demonstrate just how important respect is, even within the culture, rapper/producer Birdman walked out of a *Breakfast Club*[4] interview in 2016 because he didn't feel enough "Respek" from the co-host's questions. His raw and matter-of-fact delivery to "Put some '*respek*' on my name" went viral, with people sharing memes and videos across social media. Black Twitter timelines, especially, were filled with cultural conversations about the importance of respect for Black America. When Black America interjects the topic of respect in discussions, it reminds America and the world to:

Respect My Identity

Respect for a person's identity includes respecting their goals, hustle, dreams, aspirations, and values. The word Black automatically comes with a stigma. "There is an implicit bias and assumption that we are idiots."

Respect Where I'm From

Respect for a person's origins includes their household, community, and how things are done in that community.

Respect My Progress

We don't all have the same starting point in life or the same experiences, yet, we continue to improve ourselves as a people and as citizens of our community and country. We know far more than what society has acknowledged.

I have worked to dig deep to understand why certain stereotypes and myths continue to erroneously define and blanket Black people decade after decade and for generations without any waiver or change in perception. Why is it acceptable that those who enslaved, supported slavery, and upheld Jim Crow laws can grow into better people, while those who were affected by slavery and Jim Crow are still, to this day, being criminalized based on those unjust laws and stigmas?

For example: There is a long-standing idea that Black people are lazy, violent, criminal-minded, and less intelligent than white people. When people encounter Blacks with this "lazy" stereotype, it influences their gaze, their engagement, and judgment about that person without the courtesy of a real opportunity to discover who they are, based on authenticity and merit.

How Bias Influences the Thinking of Mainstream America

The Washington Post reviewed a survey's 2016 data and learned some not-so-surprising facts about the differences in how the different parties view race in America. The poll asked, "On average, Blacks have worse jobs, income, and housing than white people. Do you think those differences are because most just don't have the motivation or willpower to pull themselves up out of poverty?" Fifty-five percent of white Republicans agreed with this statement, while 26 percent of white Democrats believed it to be true.[5]

The truth is, upholding stereotypes is a lot easier, and perhaps even self-serving, for some than looking at truths. And when opinions are being formed about people and their culture based on stereotypes and not facts, it results in finger-pointing and blaming. In reality, *this is* what being lazy looks like.

Why We Capitalize Black

Around 2008, I began to capitalize the B in Black. There was no movement per se. I wasn't influenced by any conversations in the publishing or literacy industries (and back then, there were none). As a Boomer, I have lived long enough to witness and experience the trials of the Black community. So, every time I typed the word "Black," something inside of me nagged me to make that word count. I had long wanted the word to show up on the pages of my reports, presentations, and books as a demonstration of respect and pride for the Black community at large and for myself.

Following George Floyd's murder and BLM protests, conversations ensued on social media and reached the ears of senior editors at prominent and respected publications. *The New York Times* executive editor and Phil Corbett, associate managing editor for standards, came on board and said this in a memo to the staff:

> "We believe this style best conveys elements of shared history and identity and reflects our goal to be respectful of all the people and communities we cover." [5]

In addition to *The Times, The Atlantic, USA Today, Columbia Journalism Review,* and The Associated Press, among others, made the same call. The black-to-Black change is a big deal because it has deep roots in the culture of Black Americans, but this capitalization movement isn't new.

W.E.B. DuBois campaigned for the capitalization of the "n" in Negro throughout the 1920s, during a time when other racial and ethnic groups were written with uppercase letters, stating, "Eight million Americans are entitled to a capital letter."[7] The *Time*'s national editor, Mark Lacey, further explains the practice as "the difference between a color and a culture."[8]

Masking a Duality, aka Code Switching

Most people have different ways of presenting themselves in different situations. We behave differently at work, with friends, and with the family members who have known us all our lives. This shift is called code-switching[9]—but for Black people, it's a matter of survival and keeping their identity intact.

When you hear about or see Black people code-switching, it is for society, not us. Black Americans masks their true identity by living in dual worlds, speaking dual languages, and presenting themselves in a palatable way for white America. Thus, code-switching changes how Black people talk based on whom they are talking to. When in the presence of people who aren't Black, they tend to speak English in a way that mimics those by whom they're surrounded. It's how Black people behave in order for non-Black people to feel comfortable with us and for us to feel less judged by others.

For example, Black people speak what has been formally coined as African American Vernacular English, (AAVE). But this dialect has been portrayed as a lesser form of English rooted in stigmas of being ghetto and uneducated, also called "Ebonics," which is considered a racial epithet by some. As a result, they code switch in the workplace and, when conducting business to sound differently to be accepted and included. Yet when Black people are with other Black people, they often communicate in whatever way is natural to them, feeling more relaxed and free to be themselves.[10]

When code-switching becomes inauthentic and involuntary at work, it can have a detrimental effect on Black employees (and other people of color). That's because, essentially, they're feeling: *"There's no place here for me to be me."* In his article for *Forbes*, Dhru Beeharilal writes:

> "Whether done with conscious intent or habitually, it has been shown that code-switching can be a source of frustration, strain and burnout for minorities who recognize the perils of failing to switch—a lapse that can lead to negative consequences."[11]

Badge Value Helps Black Americans Show Up Better

Many industry leaders smirk at the term badge value. They consider the idea of badge value as old school and irrelevant. Part of this is true. The terminology has been around for decades, but it is far from being irrelevant. Badge value is still germane to how the Black community wants to be perceived. When the Black community steps out into the world in their brown skin, it's game on! Given that the nucleus of the Black experience is to constantly, daily, counter negative stereotypes, badge value provides an opportunity for Black people to portray how they want to be perceived by society—consciously and unconsciously.

The reason why premium brands, luxury cars, high-end fashions, jewelry, and alcoholic beverages are particularly important is that these things are associated with class and high value. Black people want to counter society's perceptions (and their own) about owning things that are supposed to be out of reach. They want to be seen as having class and being of value. Cross-generationally, youth and elders, notably working-class Blacks, emphasize looking their best for reasons deeply rooted in their history. It may seem shallow at first glance, but it is a genuine attempt to counter negative stereotypes.

Smoldering Coals: The Pain and Shame that Lies Deep

"Why do Black people vandalize their communities, especially during protests?"

It's the question that is often sent to me by white colleagues via email. It's rarely asked in person or publicly (after a presentation or on a blog post) for fear of being confronted as sounding insensitive, ignorant, or racist. It often feels rhetorical as most who ask have an answer they are comfortable with. As vandalism and violence became the lead headlines across the nation during the Ferguson/Micheal Brown and BLM/George Floyd protests, ALL Black protestors were described in mainstream and social media as thugs, criminals, or looters despite the majority who were peaceful protestors. Stereotyping. That's the rub.

Smoldering Coals represent the deeply rooted, deeply seeded pain from the historical legacy of slavery and its impact on America's psyche and the Black experience. It is a metaphor that I created to help explain how an unfortunate incident becomes a spark that can motivate one to peacefully protest, for example, or ignite the fury of frustration from a demoralized community.

I am not condoning violence and vandalism. If I were a retail business owner, and someone or a group of people were destroying or defacing my property, I would protect my property and call the police. Yet, understanding "the why"—evidence of human depravity and terrible community conditions, and who is actually committing the violence—is critical to understanding how peaceful protests often turn violent.

First, not all protestors are vandals.

There are traditionally two unapologetically Black non-conformists mindsets: Those who are Black and proud from sun-up to sundown and who are equality-focused. These are the majority of Black peaceful protesters. They are not passive in the fight for equality. They are thoughtful, strategic, forward-thinking, and forward-moving. Most fully embrace "peace" and are not at all likely to change mid-stream during a protest, from peacefully protesting to vandalism. *The New York Times* and cell phone tracking services have estimated that the wave of protests that started after May 25, 2020, through to the end of the year was the largest mass movement in American history. Polling data confirms that. Estimates done by counting groups argue that somewhere between 7,500 to 10,000 protests occurred in the second wave of Black Lives Matter activism. That activism was also much more multiracial and much more likely to penetrate into suburban and into rural areas than had previously been the case, according to estimates, and 95-to-97 percent of those protests involved no property damage and absolutely no violence.[12]

When Black people openly protest against America's injustices, it is often perceived by white America as anti-American or anti-white; these "anti" stories are the ones that make and linger as headlines.

Andrea Boyles writes in her book, *You Can't Stop the Revolution*, about Ferguson's Black community beliefs related to the protests and vandalism following Micheal Brown's murder:

> "For days images of burning buildings and police cars dominated the news. Although the destruction was sad and certainly not condoned by the protest community, the outcry against criticism of those who had started the fires seemed to indicate that some valued property more than Black lives. The fact that some of the lost businesses were Black-owned was unfortunate as well. However, property ownership does not negate Black owners' susceptibility to broad racialized treatment, since entrepreneurship does not grant reprieves for Blackness. This situation also does not mean that Blacks aim to destroy themselves and their communities."
>
> Such a charge acts as another stereotypical conjecture, presumably used to turn a critical lens on Black and shame them into silence and inaction."

Second, other non-conformists are less proud and very angry.

Several are low-income earners living in or near depressed communities where food deserts reign over quality healthcare and successful small (Black-owned) businesses. Some are apathetic voters stuck in a cycle of lack, and some are embittered by systems that don't work in their favor and are protesting the conditions in their community. As a result, they have different motivations for protesting—consciously and unconsciously: Many who agree with our capitalistic society lash out against it, too. It's a paradoxical situation. Many who embrace the various businesses in the Black community welcome them, yet are also resentful about some businesses that do not serve the Black community well. No one condones the destruction without believing insurance would cover the losses.

In some way, the destruction level sets the imbalance between the "haves and have-nots."

Third, not all vandals are Black.

White peaceful protestors have marched with Black communities for decades. White vandals have also created destruction during these protests and have gone mostly undetected until the age of camera phones and social media.

Tay Anderson, a Black American activist in Denver, Colorado, shared a video of himself confronting a white protester who was defacing a building during the Black Lives Matter and George Floyd protests against social injustice. After the video went viral, Anderson said this about white vandalism to *BuzzFeed News*:

> "It wasn't Black and brown folks that were antagonizing the police. It was white people throwing stuff at them." He continued: "And then when they kept throwing bags of urine, cans, and water bottles, that's when the police snapped, and they started tear-gassing innocent bystanders."[13]

Accounts of stories like this rarely made mainstream headlines but were plentiful on social media. In the Black blogosphere, pictures, videos, and screenshots of tweets of white vandals were shared and re-shared about the destruction in numerous cities where large protests occurred.

Several video clips show Black protesters attempting to stop white vandals. They further explain how Black protestors are blamed and how Black lives become endangered if the police intervene.

> "Black protesters in Baltimore begged the white folks who showed up to riot to stop because the cops would end up killing the Black protesters instead of them, and the Black protesters were told, "They're going to kill you anyway."[14]

The boogaloo bois of the boogaloo movement[15] emerged as a key fraction that was infiltrating the peaceful protests and causing destruction and mayhem. Few boogaloo bois arrests were reported, and the finger-pointing for the destruction and defacing continued toward Black protestors.

THE OPPORTUNITY

Having a broader historical and cultural understanding of American-born Black people primarily provides brands with an understanding of their lives today, as seen through the perspective of the Black lens, along with an opportunity to connect with them on a deeper, more meaningful level.

Notes

1. "A Case for Reparations," by Ta-Nehisi Coates, atlantic.com, 1/27/2016

2. *Red Summer: The Summer of 1919 and the Awakening of Black America,* Cameron McWhirter, St. Martin's Griffin, 7/03/2012

3. "Black Wall Street and the Destruction of an Institution," ebony.com, https://www.ebony.com/black-history/destruction-of-black-wall-street/#axzz4di10STZG

4. *Breakfast Club:* A New York City–based, syndicated radio show popularized by its often Hip-Hop celebrity guests for its rawness and realness, is hosted by Charlamagne Tha God, and co-host DJ Envy.

5. "According to Republicans, Black People Are Stupid and Lazy," Michael Harriot, washingtonpost.com, 4/3/2017

6. "Why We're Capitalizing Black," Nancy Coleman, *The New York Times,* 7/20/2020

7. "Capitalizing the B in Black is About Respecting Black Ancestry, Culture and History," Jameelah Nasheed, *Teen Vogue,* 12/15/2021

8. "Why We're Capitalizing Black," Nancy Coleman, *The New York Times,* 7/20/2020

9. *Code-switching* is the way in which a member of an underrepresented group (consciously or unconsciously) adjusts their language, syntax, grammatical structure, behavior, and appearance to fit into the dominant culture. Source: "Code-switching: More common than you think and hurting your team," Allaya Cooks-Campbell, betterup.com, 3/1/2022

10. American Black English is regarded as a language in its own right rather than as a dialect of standard English.

11. "Code Switching & Identity," Dhru Beeharilal, forbes.com, 10/5/2020

12. "From Civil Rights to Racial Justice: Understanding African American Social Justice Movements." FPC Briefing with Dr. Alvin B. Tillery, Jr., director, The Center for the Study of Diversity on Democracy, and Associate Professor of Political Science, Northwestern University, 4/23/2021

13. "Black Protesters Who Want to Demonstrate Peacefully Are Calling Out White People Who Instigate Violence," Clarissa Jan-Liam, buzzfeed.com, 5/30/2020

14. Twitter Thread: *FreeYourMind*

15. *The boogaloo movement:* An anti-government extremist movement that formed in 2019. In 2020, boogalooers increasingly engaged in real world activities as well as online activities, showing up at protests and rallies around gun rights, pandemic restrictions and police-related killings. Most boogalooers are not white supremacists, though one can find white supremacists within the movement. *Source:* The Boogaloo Movement, (Anti-Defamation League) adl.com, 9/16/2020

4

Blind Spot #2

Privilege and the Deficit of Empathy

"To be in other people's shoes, to understand what life looks like from their . . . world is the only way we . . . will understand what they've been trying to tell us for generations. Black people aren't asking you to apologize for being born white. They're asking us to be aware that being born white gives us an artificial empowerment over those not born white. And to use that privilege to speak up for those that are not privileged . . . Our silence is not benign."
—Paul Scanlon, motivational speaker, former senior pastor,
Abundant Life Ministries, Bradford, England

We've discussed the Black Lens and the fundamentals of the Black perspective in America. Privilege, on the other hand, examines perspectives from the white lens. It is the most fundamental aspect in recognizing racism, micro-inequities, and how white Americans view the world. As the conversation around white privilege has gained prevalence in America, a call to action has also been placed on those who say they aren't racist, and those who want to embrace other fellow Americans as equal and valued.

Interestingly, privilege not only influences how white Americans see the world, it blinds them from awareness of how the world sees them, and their actions—"harmless" behaviors, like an ethnic joke in the break room, or a comment during a strategy meeting. Core American institutions, like the construct of legal, health, and educational systems are tilted to benefit a specific group who have access to the very best those systems have to offer, while others are deprived of those same benefits.

By definition, privilege affords special rights, advantages, or immunities granted or available only to a particular person or group. Over the course of time, racism and its intricate construct in the building and advancing of America as a country has morphed into a more covert practice of prejudice and discrimination, and it must be repudiated in the same way we renounce racism.

Dr. Joy DeGruy, speaker and renowned author of *Post Traumatic Slave Syndrome,* in a presentation to a group of law enforcement officers and personnel, discussed race in a way that underscored the ruinous impact of *systemic* racism. Here is an excerpt from that discussion:

> **Dr. DeGruy:** "Tell me the ways in which white racism adversely impacts the lives of Black people as a group?"
>
> Various individuals from the audience answered, "Education." "Economic employment." "Housing." "Policing." "Healthcare."
>
> **Dr. DeGruy:** "Now Black racism. Tell me the ways in which Black racism adversely impacts the lives of white people as an entire group."
>
> The room fell silent.
>
> She smiled and replied, "Thank you. . . . You see the difference in what racism is. Racism implies that you have not just prejudice, but the power to do something with that prejudice." She illustrates that as a Black person, "I could hate [a white person]. But it's not going to change whether or not you get that loan. Whereas white racism says not only do I not like you, but I am going to change the impact of where you can live."

I've often wondered if America is empathy-deficient. It is so commonplace to dismiss the struggles of working-class Americans, minorities, and immigrants that when it happens, it's rarely discussed or challenged. Can we look at the experiences of others through their lens to understand what life must be like for them and what they are feeling?

Cornel West asks: "How are the least of these doing?

Gloria Steinem reminds us: "Empathy is the basis of any social justice movement."

Empathy helps one understand the other's challenges as if they were their own. In this powerful position, one can feel and understand the position of the other and extend compassion toward the other. When empathy is absent, public service, healthcare, banking, education, justice, housing, and, yes, marketing function at suboptimal capacity, and people suffer.

> "Prejudice is equal opportunity. Everyone can be prejudiced. To be a racist, however, you need to have the power to negatively impact whole groups of people on a systemic and structural level; jobs, housing, health, education, criminal justice."
>
> —Dr. Joy DeGruy

As a Black consumer market researcher, my job, passion, and mission is to help companies and organizations make better, more informed decisions on how to recognize and celebrate Black value as a people as well as in the marketplace so that they can earn customers' loyalty and a profitable bottom line.

Beyond the bottom line, what is there to gain that is equally as important? A genuine connection with the Black community.

Another hard truth is that although Jim Crow laws, which legalized segregation and discrimination based on color, ended several decades ago, America is still largely segregated in terms of how various American cultures live, work, and socialize. Millennials and Gen Zers are starting to change America's segregated landscape. However, for the most part, Blacks stay with Blacks, whites with whites, Hispanics with Hispanics, Asians with Asians, etc. Earning, working, playing, living, and leading your lives in a genuine community with one another can bring satisfaction, enrichment, and contentment in our lives, just as it would with people from your own race. In her book, *What Does it Mean to Be White?*

Developing White Racial Literacy (2012), Dr. Robin DiAngelo writes:

"[As a white woman], I can live my whole life in segregation. If I follow [a certain] trajectory, in my good neighborhood, in my good school, my good college, and my good career . . . I could easily never have any consistent, on-going, authentic relationships with people of color, and not one person who guided me ever conveyed that there was a loss. That is to say, that there is no inherent value in the perspective or experiences of people of color."

What might your agency, leadership team, and strategic partnerships be missing out on, by missing out on Black relationships?

○   ✖

Defining the Five Steps to Empathy

Following are excerpts from Rob Volpe's book, *Tell Me More About That: Solving the Empathy Crisis One Conversation at A Time*

1. **Dismantle Judgment.** This is the biggest towering obstacle on the journey to empathy. Awareness of when we are being judgmental, what we tend to get judgmental about, and where it comes from is the first step in tearing down the wall that judgment can put up. Be mindful of the source of your judgment. If you notice a repeated pattern, there may be an injury or bias of your own that needs attention.

2. **Ask Good Questions.** Keep the questions open—don't ask questions that can be answered with a single word. Eliminate the word *why*. It puts people on the defensive and possibly shuts them down. Use *who, what, when, where,* and *how* instead. Also, start sentences with *"Tell me more about..."* and see where it takes you.

3. **Active Listening.** Body language speaks volumes, as does looking around at a person's surroundings. Listen to these cues as well as what is being spoken. Be present and use all of your senses, including your intuition, when you are talking with someone so that you can really tune in and listen.

4. **Integrate into Understanding.** Take time to make sense of it all. What have you heard? What does it mean? Remember, it's about them, not about you. This step requires you to hold potentially contradictory information side by side.

5. **Use Solution Imagination.** This is the moment when, after having taken off your shoes, you step into the shoes of someone else. Draw on everything you've heard and keep your judgment at bay. Look at an issue from their point of view. How would you respond to them?

●

THE OPPORTUNITY

Make empathy your business. Challenge yourself and your team to examine personal biases (*see The Blind Spot Test discussed in Chapter 2*) and do the work, starting with corporate policy change to a personal change in beliefs.

●

5

Blind Spot #3

Misunderstanding the Language of Black Culture

Yes, I Speak English . . . But Are You Talking to Me?

While Black and white Americans speak English, in some ways, the two communicate in very different ways. Language is paramount. Context is crucial. Let me explain . . .

I had arrived at the boardroom of a major financial services company. There were six executives and directors of the company in total also in the room. The purpose of the meeting was to appraise the strategy for effectively reaching their African American customer base. Now, for this discussion on reaching Black people, only two Black people were seated at the table: the associate director of the finance company's Multicultural Team and me.

The director of the Multicultural Team, an Asian-American woman, proposed a targeted approach for connecting with this segment of customers. However, the vice president of advertising, a white female, was against it. She believed a targeted campaign was unnecessary, and that a general-market agency could handle all campaigns for all of their customers.

She stood up. Her eyes swept the room, and she opened her arms to suggest that what she was about to say would be welcomed and profound: *"They speak English, don't they?"* The room stood silent for a few seconds following this audacious probe. Then, the conversation began.

Since that conversation more than two decades ago, I have traveled to every corner of this nation, engaging in similar conversations with business leaders from Fortune 500 corporations, nonprofit organizations, and small businesses. What that vice president said and believed echoes in nearly every research study, presentation, and workshop I conduct. It illustrates why understanding culture, community, and cultivating a relationship with customers are critical to the success of any company.

Her resistance to a targeted approach that could have ultimately won with the Black audience ended up being a misguided, tone-deaf campaign. As a result, their PR team swooped in to strategize damage control when a sound, targeted strategy could have prevented the misstep in the first place. The best approach begins with cultural awareness. And what is the most vital cultural identifier? Language!

Business leaders' idea of language as a cultural identifier is based on two beliefs and practices: If a segment speaks a different language, e.g., Latinos and Asians, a culture different from the mainstream is recognized, and in-language targeted efforts are at least considered. There is a tendency to group Black Americans together with everyone else, given that the majority speaks English.

The misperception is that Blacks are simply darker-skinned counterparts to their white neighbors, coworkers, and church members. This couldn't be further from the truth. At the same time, there are fundamental congruences between Blacks, whites, and everyone else. Being Black in America is unlike being any other race in America. Our history proclaims us different but not deficient. We are good citizens, hard-working, empathetic, and good parents who want the best for their children. We are more educated, better paid, and more influential than we have ever been, but we are not any less Black. Obtaining access to the same liberties in America does not mean Black Americans want to lose their identity and gain that of mainstream America. Code-switching, as discussed in Chapter 3 is another example of how language plays an integral part as a cultural identifier when Black people use language as a different way of presenting themselves in different situations.

Authentic voices from everyday people who become gurus are trusted. Their language is unapologetic and informative, often raw (especially among the younger segment), and always real. The rawness of their language is not fully embraced by the entire Black community or society, yet in many cases it has motivated youth to have more acceptance of themselves (*See Blind Spot #5: Unapologetically Black, page 54*) and step up their game.

The rawness of language by Black female gurus encouraged Black women to seek sunscreen to protect their skin instead of believing and relying on their natural-born melanin to protect them. I've been pleading with skincare brands for years to investigate and create a sunscreen product for darker skin that won't leave a chalky residue. When these YouTube gurus looked into their cameras and declared, *"B*tches we need sunscreen!"* The "likes" and followers increased by the thousands. The need for sunscreen message was also delivered by Black female dermatologists on this platform, who made it their business to share information often and specifically to women with darker skin. Today we have *Black Girl Sunscreen*. A few major skincare brands have launched "invisible" formulas. However, I have yet to see any of these brands targeting the Black community.

Kendrick Lamar won a Pulitzer for galvanizing youth with his raw storytelling about underserved communities (*See Cultural Shapeshifters page 89*). I'm not implying that all language needs to be raw or wretched to galvanize Black people around your brand; what matters is to understand the language, the message, and the trusted source.

Yes, we speak English, but are you talking to us?

THE OPPORTUNITY

Develop a kick-ass strategy that engages Black consumers with cultural language that uplifts and inspires. Do not slap Black cultural jargon on a product or message—authenticity rules!

Use Black language as an opportunity to understand the nuances behind the words and connect on a deeper level.

○ ✖

Black English, A Staple in American Culture, Now Elevated via the (upcoming) New Oxford Dictionary of African American English

Black American language lives in a dichotomous space in America. On the one hand, Black Americans are often credited with language influence among the larger U.S. population. According to CNN, the latest Dictionary.com-words include several from African American Vernacular English and phrases related to race and identity.

Though many words that were originally or predominantly used by Black Americans are now commonly found among the larger U.S. population—such as "woke" and "hip"—America has long looked down on Black English, associating it with poverty and crime due to racist stereotyping.[1]

Yet Black English remains a staple of American culture. A 2018 study reported by *Sage Journal of English Linguistics,* found it had an outsized impact on Twitter where: "Three of five common "patterns of lexical innovation appear to be primarily associated with African American English."

In 2004, the term "Bootylicious" coined by Beyoncé is defined as "voluptuously sexy and attractive," was added to Merriam Webster's dictionary. "Chile" is a phonetic spelling of child, representing the dialect of southern Blacks in the United States. "Woke" goes as far back as the 1920s, is a popular term used to describe: "awareness of Blackness, Black culture, and discriminatory practices." Now, nearly one-hundred years later, Florida Governor Ron DeSantis engineered and recently signed into law the "Stop W.O.K.E." Act, a title that precisely captures what the bill's architects aimed to do: stop people in Florida from speaking out in ways that challenge racism, the discussion of race, teaching U.S. African American History, and other kinds of discrimination.[2]

On the other hand, America has frowned on Black English, associating it with poverty and crime due to racist stereotyping. Yet, Black English is a staple of American culture. Linguist Tracey Weldon told *The New York Times:*

> "It is the lexicon. It is the vocabulary that is the most imitated and celebrated—but not with the African American speech community being given credit for it."

During the summer of 2022, American literary critic, American literary critic, professor, historian, and filmmaker Henry Louis "Skip" Gates, Jr. announced that he would oversee the new Oxford Dictionary of African American English as editor-in-chief. [3]

Beyond his many credentials, Gates is well-known as an African American scholar. He became popular publicly after filming and airing the ancestry stories of dozens of diverse influential people. His most extensive study, *Faces of America,* which aired on NPR in 2010, took millions of viewers deep into the past and likely fueled interest in genealogy products like ancestry.com.

Today, Gates, who serves as Alphonse Fletcher University Professor and director of Harvard's Hutchins Center for African and African American Research, proposed the new dictionary as a joint venture of the Oxford University Press and the Hutchins Center after he was approached about the representation of African American English in existing Oxford dictionaries, according to *The New York Times.*

The New Oxford Dictionary of African American English will premier in 2025.

Notes

1. "Henry Louis Gates, Jr. to oversee new Oxford Dictionary of African American English," Shawna Chen, *Axios,* 7/22/2022

2. "How Woke Went from 'Black' to 'Bad'," Ishena Robinson, NAACP Legal Defense Fund, Aug. 2022

3. "Hip, Woke, Cool: It's All Fodder for the Oxford Dictionary of African American English," by Elizabeth Harris, *The New York Times,* 7/21/2022

6

Blind Spot #4

Misunderstanding and Misjudging Black Identity

Identity is especially fundamental for Blacks in America because of their entangled history and redacted genealogy. Black Americans are a people bred in a nation whereby they're also disowned; strangers in their homeland, outliers. Blacks own the American identity and belong here, just as much as any other American. In reality, systemic constructs place Blacks at the bottom, holding the least equity, the least prosperity, and the most blame for their failures.

To understand *Us*, one must independently investigate and seek to understand Black people and their origins dimensionally rather than the flattened Cliffs Notes versions that mainstream media overplays. Stories of generational African and African American heritage were never included or were erased from American history. School children are fed particular stories of hunched, lamp-carrying slave-defying heroes and sheroes, fascinating educated negroes, and accommodating coloreds who peacefully marched for equality.

These are fragments of Black history at best. It is not the entire story, and Black identity, to be fully understood, cannot be reduced to a few pages in a schoolbook or twenty-eight days in a month—to be fully understood.

Identity for Blacks is complex and personal. We coexist on a spectrum between whispers and remnants of rich ethnological African history and contemporary American culture that we, too, helped to build.

Black American identity represents the celebration and positive evolution of how we have defined ourselves over time. Being Black encapsulates a collection of traditions passed down from enslaved matriarchs and patriarchs. It is the appreciation for mannerisms, features, and habits that, despite being deemed unfit, continues to be a source of pride. It is soul. It is flavor and spice. It's color. It's rhythm. It's loud. It's sophisticated, opinionated, and animated. It's banding together. It's entire conversations spoken through eye contact between the two of us in a room full of them.

Today it also intersects with authenticity and cultural pride. In fact, personal identity and pride have been repurposed to empower Black people and make a statement.

"What are you"? still comes up by Black and non-Black people to mixed-race Blacks. It's also still a sore spot for many. Yet, there is less stigma around being of mixed race, and we observe more conversations about it, especially in social media.

In 2020, the percentage of people who reported multiple races changed more than all the race-alone groups, increasing from 2.9 percent of the population (9 million people) in 2010, to 10.2 percent of the population (33.8 million people) in 2020. The Black or African American and some other race population increased by 722,383 people, a 230-percent change.[1]

For mixed-race adults with a Black background, experiences with discrimination closely mirror those of single-race Blacks. Among adults who are Black and no other race, 57 percent say they have received poor service in restaurants or other businesses, identical to the share of biracial Black-and-white adults who say this has happened to them; and 42 percent of single-race Blacks say they have been unfairly stopped by the police, as do 41 percent of mixed-race Black-and-white adults.[2]

Leah Donnella, an editor for National Public Radio (NPR), writes and talks about living the mixed-race life for NPR's Code Switch podcast. Hosted by journalists of color, they tackle the subject of race with empathy and humor. Donnella's father is Black. Her mother is white. She grew up fielding the "What are you?" question and shunning the "mixed race" reference. For Donnella, growing up, "mixed" was not perceived as a positive reference for people with different ethnic backgrounds.

Donnella writes for NPR about how her mom explained how some in society use "mixed" in a negative way, which can be insulting given its implications of "things being mixed up."

Her mother righted the course by further explaining that "things may be mixed up, but not people." Mixed and mixed-race has become the preferred reference for many with different ethnic backgrounds, Donella concluded.

In fact, in her article on npr.org, "All Mixed Up: What Do We Call People of Multiple Backgrounds?" Donella shares a video of mixed-race Millennials—*Evoking the Mulatto*—who discuss their experience and challenges around the evolution of references for people with different ethnic backgrounds. Yet nearly all agree that mixed or Black is their preference:

> "I could never deny my father—ever in my life. I could never deny my mother. I could never deny where I grew up."

> "Being mixed race is such an odd blend . . . being Black and white— because there is so much hatred over many years between the two."

> "I don't feel comfortable saying just "white"—That would be weird. I wouldn't feel right."

> "Black is expressive and can mean so many things, and that's so beautiful."[3]

Code-switching, mask-wearing and how we define our mixed-race selves is a way of life. These are also the stakes-in-the-ground for unapologetic and unashamed awareness that we boldly embrace today. Black Americans are becoming less and less concerned with upholding mainstream standards and more interested in Black history and everything Black culture—art, food, dance, film, beauty, activism, fashion, etc.

Black, African American, POC or BIPOC?
What are Black people called, and does it matter?

According to Nielsen's *Amplyfying Black Voices in Media,* only 32 percent of Black viewers feel representation of their identity group is accurate. This is up from 27 percent in 2021.

"How do African Americans want to be addressed?" is the number-one question asked of me by most whites. While all African Americans are Black by race, not all Black Americans are African Americans. Black American tends to be the preferred reference, as it represents a broader, global connection to Blacks worldwide. It is an umbrella description that includes Black Caribbeans and African immigrants who want to feel included in American culture while staying connected to their country or origins. There are also some historical complexities and sensitivities to break down. Let me explain . . .

Appropriate Identifiers: "What do we call them?"

To the outside world, it seems that giving people a label or a name is a solution. The rationale is: *Give them a name, and they will know—no—we will know who they are.* But Black people, as a people, are more than the sum of a given label or name.

Historically, we were Negroes, then Colored, then African American, and finally Black. In the past decade alone, the identifiers "People of Color" (POC) and "Black, Indigenous and People of Color" (BIPOC) have emerged in an attempt to embody what and who Black people are alongside other minorities. However, Black is just not that simple. We're too varied to nickname and too dimensional to flatten.

Today, it's a safe bet to stick with the racial identifier "Black American," as it tends to be the preferred reference. It is my preference, too.

Some may not embrace the racial identifier "Black" because historically, in America, the term carries an antagonist shadow by which it was and is inextricably linked to inferiority compared to the word "white." Society, during Jim Crow, for example, reinforced this idea when white-only neighborhoods, establishments, and facilities stood superior to their Black counterparts.

For example, Hollywood, modern media, and ad campaigns have often associated Black or darker-skinned talent with crime, poverty, mischief, crudeness, incompetency, and brokenness. Saviors, angels, innocents, intelligence, beauty, success, and heroes are often associated with white and lighter-skinned talent. James Brown used his music to debunk those damaging myths and characteristics related to Black people. In 1968 his single "Say It Loud—I'm Black and I'm Proud" became the Black mantra, representing pride, unity, and healing following the murder of Dr. Martin Luther King and the subsequent riots across the country.

The song opened with a funky beat and Brown, pushing out the empowering opening line, sang, *"Uh, with your bad self. . ."* and then the call and response style to implore and declare what his people, Black people, should do: *Say it Loud! I'm Black, and I'm proud!* Over and over, *"Say it loud . . ."* is repeated throughout the song and its infectious, optimistic lyrics were on the lips and in the hearts of Black folk, young and old. It was the perfect affirmation to help ease centuries of negativity associated with the word "Black." It helped us embrace the beauty and pride of being Black and being Black in America.

The phrase African American possesses a duality: it is a political label to be politically correct, except the term does not correctly identify all people of color in America. First, it is a term that U.S.-born Black Americans (those born to or descendants of Black slaves in America) ascribe to identify as having a connection to Africa without specific knowledge of which country they came from. At the same time, they identify with America as their country and their home. Others, who strongly desire not to abandon their connection to Africa, or Caribbean countries, use the term "Black." For them, it's a big deal to feel a connection to the continent and to know which country they came from. However, some African Americans have little to no connection and no desire to seek a connection to their African heritage.

Finally, you may have noticed the phrase written as African American with a hyphen and African American without. The former has a negative connotation, as it denotes a subset of Americanness, a "less than" or "other" type of quality. When compared to those who don't have to use a hyphen, the hyphen confirms a subculture, subject to substandard treatment and less value than when one could simply use *American.*

I first noticed the redaction of the hyphen when visiting the Smithsonian's National African American Museum of History and Culture in Washington, D.C., in 2016. There was no hyphen in many of the exhibits and displays where the term was used. For me, that was huge, so I took my cue from them.

Keeping this information in your fundamentals toolbox is worth noting because these insights can prepare marketing strategists for targeted messaging and language that appeals to American-born Blacks, also understanding that it may not appeal to foreign-born Blacks. Most U.S.-born Black Americans aren't offended if referenced as African American, but Black people who weren't born here may be offended by this reference. Thus, another rationale for the use of Black. It includes Black people from various backgrounds and nationalities.

African American and Black American are used throughout this book and my presentations.

POC: People of Color represents the collective group of Black, Asian, Hispanic, and Native American people. To use POC interchangeably with Black (or with any of these groups) is out of order. Swapping POC when you mean to speak to Black or African Americans minimizes Black identity and Black history.

BIPOC: Black, Indigenous, and People of Color. This is the latest and well-meaning attempt to describe the collective minority groups who have been marginalized while emphasizing Black, but I'm not a fan. Like POC, it tends to limit our individuality as a race. While there may be some similarities in experiences, my Black history differs from that of a Hispanic or Asian person.

Combining these segments to streamline research and target segmentation efforts is not okay. Sameness, in this case, is misleading, promotes ambiguity, and is inauthentic. Decision makers may think that it saves time and requires the least effort. Still, the result is almost always one or more subsegments in the multicultural category feeling unseen and undervalued.

The segments within this category are a diverse group of American or foreign-born cultures who are people with history, beliefs, preferences, and desires. Black is Black. Latina, Latina. Asian, Asian.

And just like Black folks, there are subsegments within their respective segment as well which stand to benefit from Americans better educating themselves on cultural identities, especially being that America is filled with people from all backgrounds. Japanese are not Chinese. Mexicans are not Cubans. And bi-racial Black people are Black people, too.

Everyone deserves to be recognized for who they are.

●

THE INSIGHT AND OPPORTUNITY

Black Americans are sensitive about their identity as it is connected to their history, pride, lineage, and culture. Addressing Black Americans with respect and approaching their past as something to be embraced, not erased, reinforces your intentions to align with them, and boosts their trust in you.

Putting this embracive approach into practice is lateral and can tremendously bolster workplace, marketplace, neighborhood, and public sector environments for the better.

●

Notes

1. "Improved Race and Ethnicity Measures Reveal United States Population," Library Stories, census.gov, 2021

2. Multiracial in America, Pew Research, 2015

3. "All Mixed Up: What Do We Call People of Multiple Backgrounds?," Leah Donnella, *Code Switch—Race in Your Face*, npr.org, 8/25/2016

7

Blind Spot #5

Unapologetically Black

A Movement Evolves into a Mindset and Becomes "The New Normal"

> I don't see how I can't be unapologetically Black . . . I embrace it. It's what we eat, drink, and celebrate. I embrace everything that my ancestors did so that I can be where I am.
>
> *—Millennial focus group respondent sharing what it means to be Black in America, December 2021*

Being Unapologetically Black has evolved into a mindset beyond a movement. Whereas Black has been historically attached to negativity, fueled by youths, today Black is valuable, beautiful, and celebrated. Under this movement, we see identity rising among Black Millennials and older Gen Zers and a new vanguard of Black influencers (*See Part Three: Cultural Shapeshifters*).

Importantly, these youth who embrace this mindset are less concerned about upholding mainstream standards. This mindset is permeating conversations in social and political spheres. It has its own vernacular, influences commerce, and is shaping buying habits. It is, in essence, an order of consciousness that influences the way those who embrace it lead their lives—independent of the confines mainstream has historically placed on them.

For example, FUBU (For Us By Us) is originally a fashion brand created by serial entrepreneur Daymond John. FUBU speaks to Black pride, entrepreneurship, and responsibility for creating our products for our community. Today, it also provides momentum for "Buy Black"—a movement that unites Black people to buy from Black-owned businesses. In fact, according to PEW Research with Black Americans, 58 percent agree, "buying Black" is an extremely or very effective strategy for moving Black people toward equality in the U.S.

Further, Yelp searches for Black-owned businesses were up 2,400 percent in 2020 compared to 2019, and review mentions were up 232 percent for the same time period. Not all of the searches were from Blacks, as whites were motivated to support Black businesses following the BLM and George Floyd protests for equality.

Although many Black businesses are still not solvent, an increase in support for Black-owned businesses by Blacks, especially those in Black communities, is evident, and a welcomed discussion shared on social media.

In addition to their direct contributions to the culture and conversation about equality, Black youth are flanked with support from older generations, like big brother and big sister Gen Xers, who are taking up positions in government and law enforcement, medicine, and education. Their collective, unapologetic stand feels fresher, bolder, and better.

The collective unapologetic mindset has also inspired the WOKE Movement. The two are valuably connected, yet both individually, are often misunderstood. Let me pause on the discussion about unapologetic to explain a bit about WOKE.

Being WOKE is to be aware of and actively attentive to important facts and issues, especially racial and social justice issues. The WOKE Movement IS NOT ANTI-WHITE or ANTI-AMERICAN, yet it has called attention to critically examine the broken systems of America, challenge them, and create better ones. Thus, taking a stand is the new Black intention.

Silence, indifference or political correctness may not always be the best strategy for brands who want to reach influential Black Millennials —it could cost valuable connections and customers.

Marc Pritchard, chief brand officer for Procter & Gamble, suggested that the role brands play should be to help fix the broken systems:

> "Brands can use their voice and influence to impact important matters such as gender equality, racial bias, diversity and inclusion, and environmental sustainability."

For Black youth who live an unapologetically Black lifestyle, being WOKE is a banner of ownership, bound to a staff of value and pride. It carries with it no stigma of shame or inadequacy. But instead, it stands on a resilient foundation, owing its presence to the sacrifices of previous generations.

The most obvious attribute of this mindset is the confidence, or audacity even, for Black youth and the Black community to assume value, space, and equality for themselves. As a result, Black youth are pressed to show themselves and their culture authentically: in a positive light or in some cases with all the realness of being raw. It's about showing up as they see themselves versus relying solely on the mainstream for validation.

That's why the Black traveler platform, Travel Noire; Blavity for forward-thinking Black Millennials; *Black and Married with Kids;* the Black small business platform TSP (Traffic, Sales, and Profit); the Black feminist online community, *For Harriet;* the syndicated radio show, *The Breakfast Club,* and OWN (The Oprah Network which is a mainstream network with significant Black content); are successful media outlets. It's why beauty brands like Fenty, Taliah Waajid, Black Girl Sunscreen, and Miss Jessie's have also been so successful.

Unapologetically Black is not only a slogan but a conscious mindset:

Honors the Culture: validation, value, and integrity in Blackness.

Revisits Black history.

Celebrates/Defends the Collective.

The only qualifier is to be authentically Black. This means Millennials and older Gen Zers, especially, are prone to celebrate, share and support even people whom they don't personally know—simply because they believe in supporting the collective—Black is one.

Is Socially Conscious.

Participation in community progress and social justice. It's an unspoken obligation.

Embraces Black activism and evolved Black media.

Creates spaces that previously didn't exist, e.g., evolved, raw, real Black media spaces and events; and Black social justice authors.

Has a Woke Eye on Consumership.

Seeks to find and support goods and services that give back to the community. Supports businesses and brands of color or those that demonstrate authentic DEI (Diversity, Equity, and Inclusion) and commitments and contributions back to the collective.

In many ways, the Black Lives Matter Movement, and Unapologetically Black mindset is reminiscent of the previous post-Civil Rights Movement, Black Liberation, Black Power, and Black Pride movements. With more resources and liberties at hand, Black youth are raising the bar, and influencers from the Boomer and Gen X generations together are leading their educational, economic, and social pursuits with a solid Black consciousness for their culture and all ages to follow.

The progress by Black youth and zeal for equality while embracing the unapologetically Black mindset, in my opinion, is unprecedented. I can see in the next fifty years America looking and functioning differently than it did fifty years ago. Although there are those who are trying to stop that progress, I am confident that today's youth will achieve great things.

●

THE INSIGHT

Unapologetically Black Is the New Normal

Aligning with this momentous and paradigm-shifting lifestyle—through on-point messaging, portrayal, connection, and celebration with Black consumers—demonstrates your range to speak to what matters to them.

Remember that being unapologetically Black means:

- Demonstrating a heightened zeal for equality, upheld by a generation of consumers who are less concerned about aligning with mainstream standards.

- Embracing dual beliefs that one can be both intellectually and culturally proud while also being unconventionally patriotic.

- Self-initiated and consistent interests, education, and investment in Black history and Black culture.

- Supporting the WOKE Movement, which is not anti-white or Anti-American.

- Creating spaces in consumer categories through media and messaging and leadership that previously didn't exist

●

8

Blind Spot #6

No, Virginia. We Are NOT Post Racial

Black America is Progressing, but Not Yet Equal to White America

The First Black President did not widen Black America's opportunity funnel. It was a stepping stone in the right direction, but there is more work to do in Washington and beyond.

Black Americans today are better educated, earn higher incomes, and are increasing their exposure to a broader world outside of their communities, post-Civil Rights. Yet, they are still more likely than any other segment to navigate the broken education, healthcare, housing, finance, and justice systems.

It's a vicious cycle of starts and stops rooted in systemic inequality and centuries of resentment and discrimination that has dramatically impacted Black America's progress.

Let me explain . . .

Education

Black people are more educated today than at any other time in this country's history. However, the achievement gap continues to be a major barrier to educational progress among Black Americans. Closely related to the learning gap and opportunity gap, it refers to any significant and persistent disparity in academic performance or educational attainment between different groups of students, such as white students and minorities.[1]

A major contributor to the achievement gap is standardized test scores. These scores are often the outcome of external factors: poverty, racial segregation, health, inadequate funding for schools, and cultural bias (i.e., questions that often require specific upper-middle-class white cultural knowledge). Research shows minorities' generally lower standardized test scores reflect hidden biases in test development and administration, and bias in the interpretation of minorities' scores.[2]

"Teacher blaming" has also surfaced as a contributor to the achievement gap and is often discussed in the media. Teacher blaming is not my intention. My late mother was a teacher. I have dozens of friends and family members who currently work as education professionals or are former teachers, principals, assistant principals, counselors, and district superintendents. I have much respect and compassion for educators and school administrators. Teachers, especially, are on the front lines daily. Today, it is one of the most important yet stressful, undervalued, and underpaid jobs. In addition to helping children learn, they must also be assertive to advocate on behalf of children and themselves. They must walk that fine line between being respectful in this culture of *I'm offended* and careful about how they handle every troublesome situation with a child, given America's litigious society.

During my years in the segregated south, corporal punishment kept us in line at the Black lab school I attended. If you were paddled by your teacher, a note or a call went out to your parents, and you would likely be punished again at home. Teachers had much respect and "juice." Why? Black teachers had status back in the day. It was one of the few jobs where Black people, especially women, could advance professionally. Paddling a child today would be considered child abuse and grounds for parents to file lawsuits against the school, the district, and the city.

I admire the liberal whites who decide to teach in urban schools. They likely accept assignments in these locations with a desire to make a positive impact, given the disparities in these communities. However, they are not always prepared to deal with cultural challenges. In low-income communities, home life challenges impact children's attention spans, learning power, and motivation. Cultural misunderstandings arise, and unintentional "implicit biases" unknowingly tend to affect the thoughts and behaviors of many teachers. The challenging and negative incidents from some become the face of the entire Black student population.

For example, when Black and white teachers evaluate the same Black student, white teachers are 12 percent less likely to predict the student will finish high school and 30 percent less likely to predict the student will graduate from college. I tested into a prestigious college-prep high school, yet even there, one of the white counselors discouraged students from applying to college if they had average, or a little below average, SAT scores. In addition, Black students are more likely to be suspended or expelled, less likely to be placed in gifted programs, and they are subject to lower expectations from their teachers.[3]

Representation is also lagging among public school teachers. The gap is continuously fed when thousands of candidates do not continue all the way through the professional development pipeline to join the workforce in proportional numbers each year. Falloffs occur at the point of undertaking dedicated education training and certification. Only 4 percent of recent graduates certified to teach are Black—but research shows that getting more Black teachers into classrooms would have a real impact on long-term educational achievement for Black students.[4]

Higher Education

Many Black students choose Historically Black Colleges and Universities (HBCUs). These institutions were founded on a mission to educate African Americans during a time when slavery or segregation was still legal. Many still uphold the spirit of that mission by accepting more low-income and Black students than most other institutions.[5] Over 100 nationally celebrated institutions are recognized by the Department of Education.[6] These institutions provide academic excellence and an opportunity to study in a conducive, supportive, nurturing environment. I attended Spelman College in Atlanta Georgia, right out of high school and DePaul University in Chicago later. Academics aside, I concur that

I experienced more solidarity, pride, and a sense of self at Spelman vs. DePaul.

Nonetheless, bachelor's, master's, and doctorate degrees from HBCUs are measured as having less value in the eyes of corporate America and in the workforce vs. those from other non-HBCUs.

Closing the gap

Many corporations and wealthy citizens have contributed millions to HBCUs following the BLM/George Floyd protests, which have given these institutions more national exposure and resources. As a result, enrollment is up. But, according to the Equitable Value Explorer—a tool developed by the Postsecondary Value Commission from the Bill and Melinda Gates Foundation, which shows how much value different higher education institutions offer—only 40 percent of HBCUs produce graduates whose median earnings are at least as much as a person with only a high school degree in their state, plus enough to recoup the total net cost of the degree within 10 years of starting college. Of those, only three HBCUs—Spelman College, Xavier University of Louisiana, and Albany State University—produce graduates whose median earnings are at least as much as those of other college graduates in their state. Spelman and Xavier are also the only schools whose graduates' earnings push them into their state's 60th to 80th income percentiles, at $49,625 and $52,581, respectively. These median earnings also put Spelman and Xavier students on par with the median income of white people in their state, adding another layer of economic value to their degrees.[7]

Why this matters

These examples remind us that brands' Diversity, Equity, and Inclusion initiatives must stay laser-focused on internal challenges and work to prevent and eliminate biases with regards to talent acquisition, and performance and compensation practices. It's important too that DEI departments invest in consistent learning and development and cultural insights and unconscious bias training for all staff levels.

Health and Healthcare

It is absolutely unfair that wealthy Americans get the best medical care. Black, brown, and poor people are at the mercy of a healthcare system that doesn't always view them through a lens of humanity and compassion. Rather than feeling like patients of a healthcare system where they are expecting help and quality service, these segments often feel like a nuisance.

Black Americans' distrust of the healthcare system is not only based on *The Tuskegee Syphilis Experiments*,[8] as patients, but their healthcare journey is also more likely than any other segment to be misunderstood. Healthcare practitioners do not fully hear them, and they are more likely than white patients to suffer abysmal healthcare inequalities.

To better understand the Black patient today, is also to understand their healthcare journey. Six Key Insights significantly impact how Black Americans navigate their healthcare journey. Let me explain . . .

Relationship with food

"In Black culture, we use eating as comfort. So, our foods, how we cook them are very different from our counterparts."

—Black Gen X woman, Philadelphia, Pennsylvania

Discussing the traditional Black diet almost feels like a castigation or stereotype of Black America. Higher rates of obesity and diabetes increase the risk of high blood pressure and heart disease.

Statistics show Black people face disproportionately high rates of both conditions. About 55 percent of Black adults have high blood pressure, also known as hypertension or HBP.[9] While many Black Americans are eating healthier and exercising, others are not. Those with less healthy diets tend to prefer traditional foods, and meals which often include fried foods, fatty meats, high salt content, and sweets that provide instant gratification that these consumers see as simple indulgences.

Food deserts

Despite increasing awareness of food deserts,[10] popularized by former First Lady Michelle Obama's *Let's Move* initiative to eliminate them in seven years, they continue to be prevalent in Black communities.

Given the lack of healthy food options in many Black urban and rural areas, eating processed and junk foods has become the norm, contributing to health issues—diabetes, hypertension, and heart disease. Thus, food deserts are a racial and health issue. Unfortunately, economic policies don't focus on areas with the highest need but on areas with the highest growth potential.

Walmart partnered with *Let's Move* and proposed to open 300 stores[11] in urban and rural food deserts. They exceeded that goal and opened 450 stores. However, grocers who don't have Walmart's economic power and influence won't follow suit as they face higher insurance rates and challenges securing loans in Black communities. Charity and food banks help but still cannot provide enough resources to combat this problem.

Denial

When news of the corona virus broke, initially, there were few reports about Black Americans contracting the disease. Social media chatter exposed a belief by several Black Americans that they were protected from the virus by their DNA and melanin. It was difficult for many to wrap their heads around the virus being a potential threat until the number of deaths in the Black community, especially to those with pre-existing conditions, became one of the top national news stories in the country.

Many also reject the BMI Standard (Body Mass Index is a value derived from the weight and height of a person), believing the measurement is for whites, not Blacks. While medical studies report the prevalence of obesity is higher in Blacks than whites, especially in Black women,[12] some Blacks believe the heavier weight of Blacks versus whites is a result of "heavier bones."

"When I got a check-up last time, the doctor told me I needed to lose 20 pounds because they used the same measurement that they use on white people. I'm not built like Sally next door. I'm built like me."

—Black Boomer female, Chicago, Illinois

Prevalent diseases such as hypertension and diabetes are perceived as a rite of passage.

In several Black-patient healthcare studies, many sufferers of these diseases point to genetics and generations before them suffering from the same diseases. They are often dismissive about the severity of these diseases and use the genetics or generational explanation to rationalize unhealthy eating habits and lack of exercise. Here are a few comments from several Black patients in an HMG national healthcare study:

"My dad has hypertension."

"My grandmother had diabetes."

"These diseases are often passed down through the generations."

"There's not much we can do except to accept our fate and live our lives as best we can."

Finally, there is the denial of proper healthcare by several Black Americans who believe God and Jesus will protect them and cure them of all their ills. According to Pew Research, *"Most Black adults—including many who are religiously unaffiliated—say they believe God has the power to determine what happens in the world . . ."* This belief runs the gamut of Blacks who distrust doctors, from the fear of being mistreated to those who fear hearing bad news. Additionally, when one's faith is included in a treatment plan, it can be a great motivator for staying on the path of good health, i.e., *Pray and take your meds. Pray and watch your diet. Pray for motivation to exercise more.* At the same time, Blacks tend to take this to another level by praying for God and Jesus to handle the situation while NOT doing the work required to be healthy.

Provider-Patient disconnect

Ideally, many Black patients prefer a Black doctor as they garner more trust with them. Black patients tend to have a more relevant and positive experience with Black doctors as they find them to be more understanding of Black culture and compassionate about their disease states.

In fact, Black patients say Black doctors: understand the plight of Black people and their challenges navigating the broken healthcare system; have a holistic view of Black patients medically and culturally; and are more likely to be open to non-traditional treatment options, for example, the use of herbal supplements and DIY home remedies which are prevalent in the Black community, as long as any prescribed medicine is included.

Most white doctors are well-meaning and have good intentions. However, they often fail to connect some disease symptoms with Black culture. For example, during a recent Black-patient healthcare study, a few white doctors were confused about lingering high blood pressure levels in some of their Black patients, particularly after tracking their diet and learning that the Black diet included a substantial amount of green vegetables—a variety of greens, green beans, spinach, cabbage, etc. Whereas Black doctors, familiar with how Black Americans prepare these foods, often with fatty salty meats, would know to challenge their patients and warn them about the negative effects of those meats on their diet.

During a 2019 Black healthcare study, Sickle Cell (SCD) patients spoke openly and candidly about the rigors of being misunderstood and treated poorly. Getting treatment for the disease and the pain from the disease was challenging and demoralizing. These patients say many doctors generally don't know enough about the disease. A few doctors from the same study concur and say very little information was shared in medical school about SCD. In an attempt to help doctors understand their experience, SCD patients say white doctors, in particular, dismiss patients' accounts of symptoms because they do not believe SCD patients know their bodies. Additionally, SCD patients are often stereotyped as drug seekers, not as individuals who are in pain, with some doctors even believing, *"Black people have thicker skin or a stronger metabolism and, therefore, can endure more pain."*

Limited access to quality healthcare:
"Insurance is your doctor. Whatever is covered is what you get treated for."

Equal healthcare in some Black communities remains challenging. Many Black patients would not trust the healthcare system without good health insurance. Good insurance is described as coverage for major hospital stays, ALL medications, affordable premiums, and low or no co-pays. The staggering cost of coverage has kept the number of uninsured and underinsured unacceptably high.

Of the 27.5 million people that still lack health insurance coverage, 45 percent cite cost as the reason for being uninsured. Furthermore, the Commonwealth Fund estimates that an additional 87 million people (adults aged 19 to 64) are underinsured; that is, they have coverage, but their plan leads to unusually high out-of-pocket costs relative to income which can lead to a strain on personal finances or even debt. Of these underinsured adults, 18 percent are African American.[13]

In several healthcare studies, Black patients also complain about the poor quality of hospital healthcare in their communities. Even though this was not news to the Black community, public awareness increased during peak periods of Black American COVID-19 deaths. Research studies and news stories reported an additional link to these deaths (besides chronic pre-existing diseases), citing underfunded hospitals in Black communities. At the same time, many Black healthcare consumers believe that they will not be treated equally if they travel to better hospitals outside their community.

Abysmal treatment

Accounts of the current treatment of many Black patients read like information passages from slavery when egregious treatment of Blacks was common and the law. For example:

- Black patients are more likely to have their limbs amputated vs. white patients.

- Black women are less likely than white women to receive radiation therapy in conjunction with a mastectomy. In fact, they are less likely to receive mastectomies.

- When diagnosed with bipolar disorder, Black patients are more likely to be treated with antipsychotics—medications that are ineffective with long-term negative effects.

- Black patients with heart disease receive older, cheaper, more conservative treatments than their white counterparts.[14]

One study of emergency-room records indicates that Black patients are more likely than whites to receive lower triage scores for the same complaints, meaning that triage personnel rate the complaints as less serious. As a result, fewer serious emergency room complaints translate into longer wait times. Even in case of a serious medical emergency, such as in the case of stroke, where time to intervention is critical, Blacks experience long wait times for stroke medications.[15]

Guiding The Black Community Toward Better Health

Blackdoctor.org *Where Wellness and Resources Connect*

BDO is the world's largest and most comprehensive online health resource specifically targeted to Black Americans. With a monthly reach of 30 million, BDO understands the uniqueness of Black culture—our heritage and traditions and how both play a role in Black health.

BDO provides tips, tools, and strategies and access to innovative new approaches to health information in everyday language. All of these are needed to help Black Americans break through the disparities, gain control, and live their lives to their fullest.

Blackhealthmatters.com

BHM provides information about health and well-being from a service-oriented perspective—with lots of upbeat, positive solutions and tips that include:

- Articles on **health and wellness** and the latest health and medical news.
- **Beauty and lifestyle** stories, including tips on skin, hair, and nail care; detailed pieces about the plastic surgery industry and reconstructive surgery following illness.
- **Mind, body and soul healing** to promote wellness and explore the role spirituality and inspirational techniques play in overall well-being.
- **Nutrition and fitness** to decrease dependence on dessert and snack foods; in-depth stories about why some populations have difficulty following healthy eating directives; nutrition news; fitness; ways to avoid illness through diet and exercise.

At this writing, BHM has reached over 500,000 people yearly across various platforms, including web, video, social media, and virtual and in-person educational events.

The Black Health Matters Summit is a multi-platform event featuring live Ted Talk-inspired presentations by leading clinicians and health advocates.

BHM has also partnered with the Kappa Alpha Psi Fraternity, Inc., to launch Precision Oncology, a program designed to help the fraternity build more awareness within their group about prostate cancer and other diseases that specifically impact Black American men.

Housing

The American dream of home ownership has not panned out
for many Black Americans

> "I hate making someone else rich by paying rent—the goal is to own my own property and make myself rich."
>
> *—Gen X apartment renter*

Homeownership evokes the feeling of starting a new chapter or next stage in life. A home symbolizes success, security, achievement, and a strong foundation in the Black American community.

As a result of the Fourteenth Amendment, fair housing laws were put into place to prevent racial discrimination and redlining (*refusing a loan or insurance to someone because they live in an area deemed to be a poor financial risk*) experienced by Black Americans. But many Black Americans know that those are just words on paper. While those protections are in place and many who have been discriminated against have used these laws to enforce protection, too often claims of discrimination fall on deaf ears.

High home prices and systemic racism are primary barriers preventing Black Americans from buying homes or qualifying for loans.

During the Great Migration[16] (1910–1970), as Black Americans from the south attempted to settle into large cities in the North and Northeast, landlords imposed egregious practices on Black renters. For example, renters were required to pay for all repairs, be it a broken toilet or a new roof. If unable to abide by these requirements, they were evicted. Through public policy and private action, the Black migrants were primarily segregated into neighborhoods that were almost exclusively Black. Compared to their white counterparts, Black Americans rarely qualified to buy homes in the 1950s, 60s, and 70s, and many were forced to keep renting.

According to a 2020 report from the Economic Policy Institute, only 54.5 percent of Black American households live in single-family homes, compared to 74.5 percent of white households. More recent data from Redfin shows that home prices in cities where Black Americans are likely to live rose 16 percent, surpassing suburban and rural price growth for the first time since before the pandemic.

During the 1990s, predatory loans were the catalyst for many African Americans losing their homes, and many across the United States continue to feel the effects of racist "redlining" housing policies. Since then, many from Black American communities have not been able to purchase and are still trying to recover. In fact, Black families are more likely to live near concentrated poverty areas because of long-term segregation and racist housing and mortgage policies. A Black family earning $157K per year is less likely to qualify for a loan than a white family earning $40K.[17]

Black-owned homes and properties are valued much lower than white-owned ones, even if they are in the same neighborhoods. Additionally, community organizers share how the growth of gentrification has increased property values and property taxes in once-traditional African American neighborhoods. Increasing property taxes are forcing Black Americans out. It's often the difference in whether or not a home is foreclosed.

The Bottom Line

This push-pull cycle for African American homeownership and covert discrimination has been pervasive throughout America's housing history. It has impacted the Black community in a way that keeps them from doing what they need to do to qualify for homeownership—not by accident, but by careful design. This is also the case with commercial property. In some markets, it explains how and why African Americans have been programmed and conditioned not to own, and why so many continue to rent.

Wealth and Financial Services

"Struggle is defined as not having choices. He who has choices has resources."
—Viola Davis, actor and author, *Finding Me*

Most Black Americans believe the financial industry has not provided equitable resources for them to succeed. Most have experienced systemic bias and discrimination across all industry sub-sectors, including mortgage lenders, banks, auto lenders, credit-card companies, and insurance companies.[18]

57 percent of Black Americans agree with the statement: *"My personal finances would be better off if financial services companies treated people in my racial/ ethnic community fairly,"* vs. 31 percent of the general public.[19]

Although the Black spending power reached a record $1.6 trillion in 2021, the group's net worth declined 14 percent.[20] This stat is both exciting and disturbing. At first glance, one might initially see how the stat validates Black America as a viable market segment. At the same time, one might perceive that the Black community must rethink how they spend and save money. Neither of these perceptions is wrong, yet many Black Americans get caught up in the financial industry's requirements for a successful partnership, making progress through a series of events that cause them to fall further behind. For example, Black and mainstream business leaders steer the Black community toward home ownership, given its status as the most prominent wealth builder in the Black community. However, home ownership among Blacks has fallen more than 3 percent since 2000. Among homeowners, Black families' median home value is $150,000, compared to $230,000 for white families.[21] Systemic practices like redlining, undervaluation of

Black-owned assets, and disparities in financial education continue to plague the Black community. Additionally, Black families accumulate less than $300 billion compared with white families and save $75 billion less. The wealth gap is now at more than $11 trillion.[22]

As disconcerting as the disparities are, they provide conscious and unconscious drivers related to the level of trust with financial institutions, Black progress, and Black community sustainability. Four key insights provide the backstory to the industry's blind spots about Black America's pursuit of financial progress. Let me explain each . . .

Advice and examples from Parents/Guardians/Mentors are Influencers and Black America's Legacy

Many Black savers and investors who are wealth-focused learn at a young age to be good stewards of their money from older family members—parents and grandparents or mentors. They are encouraged by these early financial influencers to begin their wealth-building journey with two critical pieces of advice:

ONE: Pay yourself first (and for the religious, pay God first, then yourself).

TWO: Invest in real estate. The elders taught them about the stability and financial strength of owning a home and additional properties.

For decades, a myth has been circulating that Black Americans reject money management opportunities.

The problem is that many current financial education programs don't necessarily address these consumers where they are. Financial literacy education is valuable when tied to culture, relevant experiences, situations, and something that matters. A few years ago, I was a presenter at a wealth-building seminar in Chicago. It was produced by WVON, a local Black talk-radio station, and held at The DuSable Museum of African American History.

The museum's auditorium seats 400 people. I was not optimistic about a great show rate, given the event was on a Saturday at 8:30 in the morning! I was shocked and delighted to see the auditorium filled and lines of people wanting to get in.

As the researcher, I interviewed a few people waiting in line. The consensus was they wanted to learn about budgeting, understand financial terminology, investing, home buying, acquiring business loans, etc. The relevancy of the trusted voice and venue also engaged attendees—Black-owned and operated WVON 1690 AM radio was the sponsoring media, and the venue was The DuSable Museum of African American History.

Relevant financial training matters

Recently, I conducted listening sessions for a prominent regional midwestern bank among Black American upper level managers. One participant shared his practical approach to the bank's financial education training. The purpose was to help middle- to lower-income Black communities make better decisions about managing money.

During his financial literacy training session, he mentioned holding up a hammer and saying: "This is a hammer. It can create and destroy." The head nods and yeses in the room confirmed that session participants were listening and in agreement. Then he said he held up a handful of dollar bills and used the same language as the hammer example. "This is money. It can create and destroy."

Before he could provide any examples to the latter statement, "The light bulb immediately came on. They got it!" said the Director. The Director further explained: "A seed was planted. What they 'got' is a better understanding of the importance of saving, and investing, home buying, and saving for the next generation, and not just buying the next new thing to make themselves feel good at the moment."

I loved it. This is what relevancy and relatability looks like and feels like.

Current underwriting is biased

Many Black banking and insurance executives understand the conservative nature of the financial industry yet agree that current underwriting practices are not poised to understand the needs and culture of the Black community.

Underwriting is the financial industry's guidelines and particular facts about people and circumstances to measure risk and set rates. For a mortgage or business loan, understanding the applicant's financial situation would typically include one's credit score, a credit report debt-to-income ratio, financial reserves for a mortgage, the type of property and units it has, etc. For decades underwriting guidelines and risk factors often include biases, significant discrepancies, and lack of consideration for circumstances and situations relevant to the Black community.

According to data recently made available from the U.S. Federal Reserve, more than half of companies that have Black owners were turned down for loans, a rate twice as high as white business-owners. The report found that while Black-owned firms were the most likely to have applied for bank financing, less than 47 percent of these applications were fully funded. Even when Black business owners get approved, their rate of failure to receive full financing is the highest among all categories by more than 10 percent.[23] And up to 95 percent of Black-owned businesses may have been shut out of the federal government's recent Paycheck Protection Program.[24]

Popular Black-owned businesses like beauty salons and barber shops, funeral homes, vegetarian and country-of-origin restaurants, etc., are often perceived to have higher risks, unscrupulous business practices, and create a great deal of suspicion within underwriting. Thus, they are denied loans and appropriate, affordable insurance coverage. Black and brown industry executives challenging underwriting, and the national attention on the movement for racial justice, are both signs that financial industry regulators are accelerating their focus on potentially discriminatory underwriting practices. Hopefully, underwriting will get a re-do, not a tweak. It's about understanding the who and the why.

Wealthier Black Americans have a different story from wealthier whites. They are Black community financial influencers and under the financial industry's radar.

Society and business leaders often overestimate the progress of Black America by focusing on wealthy entertainers, sports figures, politicians, business leaders, physicians, etc. They miss some staggering disparities. Black households account for 13.4 percent of the U.S. population yet hold just 4 percent ($4.6 trillion) of total household wealth vs. white households. White households account for 60 percent of the U.S. population and hold 84 percent ($94 trillion) of total household wealth in the U.S.[25]

Researchers suspect that the answer partly has to do with how little exposure Americans have to people who are unlike themselves. Given how economically and racially segregated the country remains, many Americans, especially wealthy whites, have little direct knowledge of what life looks like for families in other demographic groups.[26]

There is a vast disconnect between how Black people describe and feel about wealth versus whites. The outcome from questions shared with Black and white adults during qualitative and quantitative surveys delivered wealth descriptions of very high living: owning yachts, islands, and traveling around the world, etc., are wealth descriptions provided by both Black and white respondents. Some Black respondents, however, are more likely than whites to describe wealth as not having to worry about the essentials or immediate needs: being debt free, and being able to afford a comfortable home, an automobile, college tuition for their children, and money for travel.

During focus group discussions with Black affluents, there is a sense of hesitancy about fully embracing the idea of wealth, especially when asked, *"Are you wealthy?"*

Most of the consistent savers and investors declare when it comes to wealth, they are not there yet. Reasons given include: not being satisfied with their current portfolio fund balances, and the notion that wealth conveys a very high standard of living—owning a yacht, 3 to 4 homes, or homes in another country etc. Some express subconscious guilt about having more money than family and friends.

Ghetto fabulous

Chris Tucker's character, "Carter" in the original *Rush Hour* movie describes his one-time wealthy showy, ostentatious lifestyle as *living ghetto fabulous*. Ghetto fabulous might include a luxury car, maybe not the latest model, but in mint condition; the latest fashion styles for sure including a few pairs of shoes and accessories from designer brands like Gucci and Louis Vuitton; a 4-to-5-bedroom home, not elaborately furnished but with a few bells and whistles to generate "oohs" and "ahhs" from your posse; several thousands of dollars in the bank and a few hundred in your pocket, and being able to order that expensive steak without a second thought. It's different from "white wealth," but not deficient.

Against a backdrop of dismal economic stats mentioned earlier, all is not lost. Wealth-management studies that my company conducted with Black affluents over the years, reveals hope and optimism about the Black community making wealth gains. Wealth over time is accumulated and passed down differently in the Black community vs. the white community. The important point is that it's happening and unfortunately, rarely reported. Many of the experiences from Black affluents are positive yet are contrary to what is seen and heard in the media.

Black Affluents are disciplined savers and investors

Many Black Affluents forego the purchase of a lot of material items and instead focus on the bigger opportunity to save and invest for a comfortable, worry-free future for themselves and for the next generation. Most also built their wealth via matching employer-contributed 401K accounts and having "side hustle" businesses. They are consistent contributors as well as to a variety of wealth products that include: stocks, bonds, traditional and Roth IRAs, traditional savings, REITs, real estate, CDs, 403b, 457 plans, and more.

Few claim to have contributed to their portfolio via an inheritance. In 2019, thirty percent of white households had received an inheritance at an average of $195,500 compared to only 10 percent of Black households at an average of $100,000.[27]

Generational wealth is on their radar

The African proverb, "Each one teach one" is often perceived as an unspoken obligation of Black Affluents. The primary charge for financially knowledgeable and wealthy Blacks is to educate their children, family members, and help others in their community learn about wealth-building strategies. Ensuring wealth transfer from Black Affluents to their families is an essential goal of investing.

Black youth, Millennials, and older Gen Zers are also teaching their parents about wealth management, entrepreneurship, and investing.

In fact, there is growing interest among Black Americans in participating in the stock market, and there's evidence that Black Americans are beginning to close the investment gap, according to the Black Investor Survey 2020 conducted by Ariel Investments and Charles Schwab.

Younger Black Americans appear to be driving that shift. The report found 63 percent of Black Americans under the age of 40 participate in the stock market, on par with their white counterparts.[28]

At the same time, Black affluents have no shame in scolding those who get caught up purchasing material items with no long-term value.

Observing poor money management behavior in others has motivated many to prioritize generational wealth declaring, for example: "I'm making sure that I am passing (my wealth) on to my children." Or, "I'm leaving a certain percentage to my nieces and nephews with stipulations—finish college, continue to save and invest and pass on to the next generation."

Unjust Justice

Justice is an umbrella term associated with many categories, i.e., economic, political, criminal, personal, organizational and workplace, communicative, family, social, etc. In fact, too many to discuss here. Broken justice is ubiquitous. It exists in every category and has impacted every ethnic group in America, especially Black Americans.

For Black Americans, social justice is the battle cry of those who have found their lives, their loved ones, and everyone who looks like them at the mercy of criminal justice in the United States. Social justice is at the core of our humanitarian exigency, and broken, discriminative criminal justice is an unmerited, yet normalized, way of life.

Centering social justice in the spotlight, I'm interested in examining the fair and equitable distribution of resources, wealth, opportunities, and privileges in society. The United States criminal-justice system is designed to deliver "justice for all." That means enforcing laws, ensuring public safety, and delivering justice to those who have committed crimes. It also means providing a fair justice process.[29]

The history of American racism and discrimination has carried over into today's modern justice systems, and while historically, punitive actions against Black people were blatantly racist, today, they're more obscure, even when only thinly veiled. The statistics are there, however, and the numbers tell a story of inequality. Especially among Black men, the justice system is a near-indomitable way to perpetuate unjust treatment in this country. And there's a reason: political power, and media.

The media is largely responsible for shaping and promoting negative images of Black Americans. For example, too often, first thoughts and biased mindsets about Black men are typically negative: i.e., deadbeat dads and criminals. These mindsets contribute to Black men being one of the media's most vilified personas and segments.

In our own communities, we witness how some Black men have coped with this weight, by acting out their pain and anger, and by making poor choices. Those choices are almost always translated to an overarching image of the Black community as problematic and troublesome—thus having less value in the eyes of mainstream America. This mindset creates biases that point to some of the contributing factors as to why Black America has a harder time with the justice system. It's a troublesome cycle.

Data about unjust social and criminal justice against Black Americans is overwhelming. In addition to the discussion about the broken systems in general, below are a few data points from several studies and social justice organizations that report on criminal and social injustices and how discriminatory practices impact the ongoing struggle for equality by Black America:

- Only 70 of the 3,843 people who have ever served as federal judges in the United States—fewer than 2 percent—have been Black women.[30]

- Sixty-five percent of Black adults have felt targeted because of their race. Similarly, approximately 35 percent of Latino and Asian adults have felt targeted because of race.[31]

- Criminal justice policies often result in the disproportionate incarceration of Black Americans. Black people are incarcerated at more than 5 times the rate of whites.[32] Prison reduces their participation in the political process.

- The Sentencing Project found that roughly 20 percent of Black male prisoners serve life sentences. According to the study, about 11 percent of Black women serving prison sentences are also serving life. Black women represent more than 50 percent of women serving life without parole (LWOP) sentences.[33]

- Black women account for one-third of women serving life sentences and virtual life sentences in the U.S.

- One of every 39 Black women in prison is serving life without parole, compared to one of every 59 imprisoned white women.

- As of 2020 Black women account for 25 percent of the women on death row and are confined in the following states: Alabama, California, Florida, Georgia, Louisiana, North Carolina, and Texas.[34]

The widespread "deadbeat dads" image has impacted divorce and child custody laws and processes. They are enforced with different criteria for Black men. In fact, many lawyers are biased against Black fathers.

Unconsciously and consciously, many lawyers fail to uncover enough of the history and involvement Black fathers have with their children.

While the current judicial process hinders Black men, Black women move ahead faster, as better-educated and higher-income earners and move into the matriarch position of the family. Family dynamics and traditional roles are challenged, which makes divorces different in the Black community.[35]

Black men are more likely to be falsely accused of family offenses. The implicit biases of the police officers and judges involved in these cases assume that the Black man is probably guilty of the offense; Black men are more likely than Caucasians to get arrested, with temporary orders of protection granted based on little or no evidence. This is a huge fear that deters Black men from filing for custody; they fear the retaliation of a false allegation and the many ways such an allegation could destroy their lives.[36]

At the same time, as some attention shifts towards the many good fathers that we know, we see these fathers emerging as custodial parents, whereas historically mothers used to get custody in most jurisdictions automatically.[37]

THE OPPORTUNITY

It's good to observe and acknowledge the socioeconomic progress that Black Americans have achieved over the last sixty years. But it's also important *not* to replace that progress with indemnification. Black Americans are still navigating deeply rooted systemic challenges.

Fully, 63 percent of Americans are concerned about systemic racism and racial justice. To face it, brands have an opportunity to step up as an ally for equality, equity, and inclusion both in and out of the workplace.

Notes

1. The Achievement Gap defined, The Glossary of Educational Reform

2. "Rethinking Standardized Testing from an Access, Equity, and Achievement Perspective: Has Anything Changed for African American Students?," Michael Couch II, Marquisha Frost, J. Santiago and Adriel Hilton, *Journal of Research Initiatives,* 9/9/2021

3. "Inequality at School: What's Behind the Racial Disparity in our Education System," Kristen Weir, American Psychology Association, Nov. 2016

4. *AdAge,* "The Economic State of Black America: What is and what could be," McKinsey Global Institute, 6/17/2021

5. "Examining the Economic Value of an HBCU Degree," Mirtha Donastorg, The Plug, 12/1/2021

6. "Black Brilliance: Why Investing in HBCUs Is the Smart (and Right) Thing to Do," Kelsea Johnson, IFY.com, 8/18/2021

7. "Examining the Economic Value of An HBCU Degree," Mirtha Donastorg, *The Plug Podcast,* 12/1/2021

8. The Tuskegee Syphilis Experiments were conducted between 1932 and 1972 by The United States Public Health Service. The study initially involved 600 Black men—399 with syphilis, 201 who did not have the disease. Participants' informed consent was not collected. Researchers told the men they were being treated for "bad blood," a local term used to describe several ailments, including syphilis, anemia, and fatigue. In exchange for taking part in the study, the men received free medical exams, free meals, and burial insurance. Source: CDC.gov

9. High Blood Pressure Among Black People, American Heart Association, https://www.heart.org/en/health-topics/high-blood-pressure/why-high-blood-pressure-is-a-silent-killer/high-blood-pressure-and-african-americans

10. *Food deserts:* The USDA defines a food desert as a place where at least a third of the population lives greater than one mile away from a supermarket for urban areas, or greater than 10 miles for rural areas. By this definition, about 19 million people in America live in food deserts that disproportionately impact Black and brown people. Source: "Why Food Deserts Are Still a Problem in America," cnbc.com, 8/20/20

11. "Walmart to Open 300 Stores in Food Deserts," businesschef.com, 5/19/2020

12. Differences in Weight Perception Among Blacks and Whites, National Library of Medicine, 12/20/2011

13. Racism, Inequality, and Health Care for African Americans, TCF.org, Dec. 2019

14. "The State of Healthcare in The United States Racial Disparities in Healthcare," *Human Rights Magazine,* vol. 43, no. 3, americanbar.org, Jan. 2023

15. "Black Americans don't trust our healthcare system—here's why," thehill.com, Aug. 2017

16. *The Great Migration:* Six million African Americans left the Jim Crow South for northern cities of the U.S., is a key way in which Black American families tried to improve their economic standing, from 1910–1970. "Segregated Housing Markets and the Erosion of Black Wealth: New Evidence from Pre-war Cities," voxeu.org

17. The Century Foundation

18. "Black spending power reaches record $1.6 trillion, but net worth falls," cnbc. com, 2/14/2022

19. "Addressing Racism in America's Financial System," Lisa Osborne, edelman.com, 8/05/2021

20. *Ibid.*, cnbc.com, 2/14/2022

21. "Black-owned businesses in U.S. cities: The challenges, solutions, and opportunities for prosperity," Andre M. Perry, Regina Seo, Anthony Barr, Carl Romer, and Kristen Broady, brookings.edu, 2/14/2022

22. *Ibid.* cnbc.com, 2/14/2022

23. "Black-owned firms are twice as likely to be rejected for loans. Is this discrimination?," Gene Marks, theguardian.com, 1/16/20

24. Center for Responsible Lending

25. "The Black and White Wealth Gap Left Black Households more Vulnerable," Second quarter 2020, brookings.edu, 8/12/2020

26. "The Upshot: Whites Have Huge Wealth Edge Over Blacks (but don't know it)," Emily Badger, *The New York Times*, 9/18/2017

27. "The Black-white wealth gap left Black households more vulnerable," Emily Moss, Kriston McIntosh, Wendy Edelberg, and Kristen Broady, brookings.edu, 12/8/2020

28. "Young Black Americans are closing the investment gap, but other financial disparities remain," Kristen Beckman, ALM benefitspro.com, 3/25/2021

29. Goodwin.edu 5/4/2021 and 8/5/2020

30. "Black women account for a small fraction of the federal judges who have served to date," John Gramlich, Pew Research Center, 2/2/2022

31. Race and Justice, naacp.org

32. "The Color of Justice: Racial and Ethnic Disparity in State Prisons," Ashley Nellis, Ph.D, *The Sentencing Project*, 10/13/2021

33. "Two-thirds of Prisoners Serving Life Sentences Are People of Color," Aris Folley, thehill.com, 3/02/21

34. "Extreme Sentences Disproportionately Impact and Harm Black Women," Trevarian Mason, The National Black Women's Institute, 9/23/2021

35. "9 Interesting Facts About Divorce for Black Couples," Charreah K. Jackson, *Essence Magazine,* 10/28/20

36. Familylawyermagazine.com, 7/14/2020

37. *Ibid.*

9

Blind Spot #7

Generations of Awakenings Give Rise to the Fight for Equality

I was surprised to learn that the definition of equality may be different depending on who you ask.

If you are familiar with the speeches of Dr. Martin King, Jr., then you're familiar with his stance on equality. He spoke about it all the time in his metaphors, speeches and commentary. Dr. Joe Feagin, the Ella C. McFadden Professor and Distinguished Professor of Sociology at Texas A&M University who has conducted extensive research on racial and ethnic studies, gender relations, and the urban political economy, made a compelling argument for defining the word "equality" differently between Black and whites in America:

> ". . . of the many times (ML) King spoke of structural changes needed to achieve equality . . . first and foremost [is] the need for white and Black people to agree on what "equality" actually means."

They noted that in King's speech, a major problem in getting white people to understand the meaning of the Civil Rights Movement was understanding that:

> "There isn't even a common language when the term "equality" is used. . . . Many white people, even well-meaning people, think that equality means Black people have to improve."

Feagin goes on to say:

"White people . . . have most of the political and social power to change that racial discrimination and inequality now."[1]

According to Gartner Research's Annual Values Study, equality is reported as the #1 value for Black people year after year. Equality is typically ranked lower, on average #8 on value, for whites.[2]

Black Americans have spent generations seeking equality, working for it, and fighting for it. White Americans don't worry about equality as much because they don't have to.

There's an interesting dichotomy here: America prides itself on history as a source of inspiration and a base to examine and measure growth from trials to triumph. Yet, America refuses to examine the whole story of its unbridled history and thus will never be able to make amends for all it has done. I've heard: *"We don't want the founding fathers to look bad."* Or, *"We don't want to upset white children."* For generations, Black parents have had to swallow their pride and muster up the courage to look their children in the eye, to have "The Talk" about race and racism. What type of future America are we creating when white parents choose legislation that erases Black history rather than having their version of "The Talk?"

From Reconstruction to Post Civil Rights and intergenerationally, the most important achievement for Black people who ushered in movements that defined their era was a fight for equality:

The Silent Generation (b.1927–1946): Endured the full effects of Jim Crow laws. Solidarity empowered the culture, emphasizing the common goal for equality.

Boomers (b.1947–1964): The 1955 murder of 14-year-old Emmett Till inspired the Civil Rights Movement. Subsequently, there was the emergence of The Black Power Movement.

Gen Xers (b.1965–1980): Post Civil Rights, the continuance of Black Power Movement and challenging the realities of racism and discrimination.

Millennials (b.1981–1996): Trayvon Martin's murder and the George Zimmerman verdict spurred the WOKE Movement[3] Black Lives Matter, Dream Defenders, Million Hoodies in the Hood, etc., and a new generation of Black social-justice leaders.

Gen Zers (b.1997–2012) Elder Gen Zers became aware of inequalities following George Floyd's murder and support Black Lives Matter protests against social inequities.

These awakenings happened during moments of fear not to anger white America to civil injustice, yet are in response to Black Americans and their supporters taking a stand. Demonstrations and protests were Black Americans and supporters way to take a stand—and they worked! These movements produced significant influence to demand legal change and set societal precedents.

What is Equality and Equity?

Equality: Equal opportunity.

Equity: Providing what is needed for equality/equal opportunity.

Race, fairness, equality—these conversations are taking place daily, at home, and in the Black community. One tool that Black youth has used in their pursuit to have a voice in America, is social media. Moving hashtags and timelines from a thought, to an idea, to a trending phenomenon is quite comfortable for these digital natives. #BlackLivesMatter, #TakeaKnee, #Staywoke are examples of how those racial conversations once confined to our kitchen tables, have taken up space in cyberspace and sparked more in-person conversations that speak out against injustice. There was never an intention for these platforms to be anti-white, anti-flag, or anti-American. They were created to be pro-equality, pro-inclusivity, and yes, pro-Black. Megastar Beyoncé delivers a spot-on comment that encapsulates this insight perfectly:

"It has been said that racism is so American, that when we protest racism, some assume that we are protesting America."

The CROWN ACT

Creating Respect and Acceptance as Normal for Natural Hair

The CROWN ACT, which stands for "Creating a Respectful and Open World for Natural Hair," is a law that prohibits race-based hair discrimination, which is the denial of employment and educational opportunities because of hair texture or protective hairstyles, including braids, locs, twists or Bantu knots. In other words, Black people can go about living their lives, like everyone else in America, wearing their hair and without fear of being sent home, suspended or reprimanded in schools or the workplace.

The Official Campaign of The CROWN Act is led by the CROWN Coalition, founded by Dove, The National Urban League, Color of Change, and The Western Center on Law & Poverty.

— BLACK AMERICANS IN CONTEXT —

THE EQUALITY PARALLEL

#BLACKLIVESMATTER
#GEORGEFLOYD
#BLACKGIRLSCODE
#OSCARSOWHITE
#TAKEAKNEE
#STAYWOKE
#UNAPOLOGETICALLY BLACK
#GROWINGUPBLACK
#BLACKGIRLMAGIC
#MELANINONFLEEK
#PROUDTOBEBLACK
#1000BLACKGIRLBOOKS
#BLACKTHERAPISTSROCK
#THERAPYFORBLACKGIRLS
WWW.PEPPERMILLER.NET

- For years, obtaining Equaltity has been the #1 value for Black Americans

- Equality was rated far less important for whites— it's last reviewed ranking was #8. Ranked #1 for whites was Loyalty.

It was created in 2019. Of the 19 states and 41 municipalities that have individually adopted the legislation, there are racial- and gender-minority lawmakers, partnered with white lawmaker allies, who have pushed to move the bill forward. In the public sector, Dove and its partners have collaborated with lawmakers to sponsor the bill and its message.

Although the act passed the House of Representatives earlier this year, unfortunately, at this writing, the bill did not pass the Senate and will need to be re-introduced during the 2023 legislative session.

Addressing beauty equality in retail

I conducted qualitative research for a number of Black and mainstream hair-care-product manufacturers whereby select respondents from previously held focus groups from the same study also participated in shop-alongs in various big-box and major drugstores. In several situations, the hair-care aisles featured entire aisle-length displays of general market hair-care and beauty products. Black and ethnic hair-care products were almost always a fractional section of products. Importantly, the mainstream hair-care and beauty product aisles are typically labeled "Beauty Aisles" vs. the labeling for ethnic aisles where the word "Beauty" is excluded. What message does this send to Black and minority consumers?

THE INSIGHT

The Black agenda is simple: inclusion, equality, and fair treatment. When these ideals are promoted and proclaimed, those in power challenge them. White America does not need the type of equality that Black people seek. Therefore, equality is not a priority for them.

THE OPPORTUNITY

Approach equality with empathy because inequality is not an imagined state—this is how one becomes aligned and allied with Black Americans. The methods by which Black people protest to communicate the urgency of equality do not have to be understood, accepted, or approved by white America. The message needs only to be effective and heard.

Notes

1. "What Martin Luther King, Jr. Said About Systemic Racism," *Texas A&M Today*, 1/15/2022

2. Source: Gartner Values Research, 2017

3. *Woke/Woke Movement:* Aware of and actively attentive to important facts and issues (especially issues of racial and social justice)

PART THREE

Cultural Shapeshifters

The Rise and Rebirth of Black Influence:
Black Youth | Black Women | Black Men
Black Immigrants | Black LGBTQ+ Supporters

Who are the Cultural Shapeshifters?
Exploring the Five Highly Influential Go-To Segments
Redefining Cultural Norms

Cultural Shapeshifters are the "now" generation. They're composed of a multigenerational group of socially, economically, and politically progressive Black Americans responsible for redefining cultural norms and ushering in the Unapologetically Black lifestyle within the last decade. Their undeniable influence, be it starting trendsetting grassroots movements, changing the standards, or launching massive global crossover brands, is why they're the industry's go-to segments, especially Black youth: Millennials and (elder) Gen Zers.

I used the collective segment "cultural shapeshifters" because they're reshaping what it means to be Black in America in all the ways that matter most: they're more educated, more economically enterprising, more politically involved, more culturally conscious and more globally mobile than any other preceding generation. Their place in American society is far from equal, but further along than generations past. As consumers, their spending power in the market is important to any mainstream brand's success, yet they are generally nonexistent on the mainstream stage. Where's the representation? The "swap out," a marketing ploy whereby minority talent is swapped interchangeably with white talent, is not representation. The Unapologetically Black fanfare was created to fill that representation gap. Targeting the Black dollar makes sense, but the underrepresentation of Black people in an authentic, positive light has always been a problem. In their own way, in their own voice and within their own communities, Black Youth, with older generations following, are solving that problem by creating products, services, and platforms to represent themselves. We'll explore what they're doing to close the gap and how they're doing it, in the next chapter. Let's examine who these subsegments are.

Among the Cultural Shapeshifters are multigenerational and demographically diverse subsegments. You'll see they're not all the same. They lead unique lifestyles, and there are nuances to their identity that are important to recognize. But they collectively identify as Black: African American, Black American, Black, African, Afro Latinx and Afro Caribbean.

There are five subsegments, ranked by level of market influence:

Black Youth, "The Forerunners" is the most influential subsegment made up of Millennials and Gen Zers. They are the industry's go-to segment.

Black Women, "Fighters for the Cultural Good" are statistically the largest share of household leaders and providers, and the most educated subsegment.

Black Men, "The Path Forgers" are the freshest subsegment to positively redefine their reputation and stance in the Black community and American society.

Black Immigrants, "The Foreigners Only by Name" is a subsegment of first- or second-generation Black transplants who share in the struggles of the Black American experience, and contribute to the culture in meaningful, groundbreaking ways.

Black LGBTQ+, "The Fairness Fighters" are individuals living and striving for fairness via their contributions to Black and LGBTQ+ equality, and the equality movement overall.

Black Dimensionality

Black feminist scholar Kimberlé Williams Crenshaw, law professor at Colombia and UCLA, coined the term **intersectionality** in 1989 as a qualitative framework to identify and study the overlapping social identities of people in minority groups who are empowered or disempowered as a result of their race, gender, class, sexual orientation, religion, and other individual characteristics—and at the point where these identities meet. For example, women are marginalized based on gender, but Black women are marginalized based on gender, and marginalized again, based on color. Black LGBTQ+ people are marginalized, too, based on gender, skin color, and sexuality. The early twentieth century Women's Suffrage Movement won women the right to vote, as well as other constitutional protections, but that movement and those privileges narrowly included Black Women. These intersections underscore the proverbial hoops those in minority classifications find themselves having to jump through, just to be recognized, respected and celebrated as equal.

Black **dimensionality** is another way to say that Black people (and people of color) are not a monolith and should not be categorically clustered into one group. In addition to intersectionality, Black dimensionality examines the range in which Black American identity exists. The five subsegments above are a glimpse of that range. Even within those subsegments are sub-identities made up of any number of qualities. What this means is that to effectively survey Black American consumers, researchers and leaders must understand the dimensionality of Black American identity. The most basic example of this is assuming a dark-skinned person is a U.S.-born African American when that person could be of another nationality. Let's say I invited a group of seven Black adults over age 45 and living in Chicago and Washington, D.C., to participate in a public transportation case study. Their task would be to share their opinions and suggestions about new plans to expand public transportation in the city. I can guarantee seven completely different personal and cultural responses based on their youth and early adulthood, family, community, and their varied backgrounds in education, careers, and leadership.

The problem with race in America will always be a paralleling component, centric to each grouping of individual experiences, which influence beliefs and thus habits and behaviors. Each generation, as explored in these next chapters, endured new and unchartered territory in America. Each generation brings a unique set of experiences that has made Black culture what it is.

I explain the critical need for leaders to hire Black researchers and experts in Part Four of this book, "Rethinking Black: Relationships, Community, and Representation." The takeaway now for Black Dimensionality, however, is to look past skin color, and seek to understand to whom you are really talking.

10

Black Youth: The Forerunners

Self-Made, Highly Influential, and Not as Mainstream as Some Think

Forerunners are people who represent the coming or development of someone or something else and this definition couldn't be a better description of Black youth in America today, especially innovative and enterprising Black Millennials. Their unique dimensionality empowered them to reshape and forge a culture of Black Excellence in a single decade.

So, who are Black Millennials and Gen Zers? They undoubtedly have many characteristics in common with mainstream white Millennials and Gen Zers. They're not completely different. At a glance, most Millennials and Gen Zers are:

Digital natives: They grew up almost exclusively having access to and their lives shaped around the internet, mobile phones, and social media.

Comfortable with race and differences: They embrace diversity—including race, skin color, gender, religion, sexual and gender identity, disabilities, and other characteristics.

Deeply connected with brands that provide value and personal ties to their communities.

Loyal to a cause: if you give them a reason to be so.

Seekers of equality.

According to estimates from the U.S. Census Bureau, in 2019, Millennials bypassed Baby Boomers as the nation's largest living generation, 72.1 million to 71.6, respectively.

Most Millennials and Gen Zers
Desire a Nation of Equality

♀ An Unequal Society	♂ For Equality
• 60% of Gen Zers and 56% of Millennials see systemic racism as very or fairly **widespread** in general society • 1 in 5 Millennials believe they are discriminated in the workplace "all the time." • Two-thirds of Millennials and Gen Zers see **wealth and income as unequally distributed** in society.	• 68% **want more inclusive topics in their college curriculum** • 48% of Gen Zers and 47% of Millennials approve of gay and lesbian marriage • 59% of Gen Zers say that **data collection profiles should include additional gender options** • Gen Zers and Millennials **support single women raising children on their own**

Source: Pew Research, 2021

Fully 72 percent of Black Gen Zers are Black and proud, and they want to see reframed stories of Black history that depict historical resilience, modern-day Black excellence, celebrations of Black achievements, and Black culture in schools.[1]

But the nuanced ways in which young Black individuals do differ are essential. Exploring these nuances and often unrevealed insights can guide decision-makers' understanding of who this segment is and how to communicate with them most effectively. If leading brands can win their attention and advocacy, perhaps they may win their loyalty.

Black American Millennials are a large and diverse group—the oldest of whom have grandparents who were coming of age during the Civil Rights Movement and the deaths of Martin Luther King, Jr. and President John F. Kennedy. The youngest Millennials would have been sixteen years old when George Zimmerman murdered Trayvon Martin in 2012. Millennials are more socially adaptable than any of their generational predecessors; they live, work, shop, and interact in mainstream America more than their parents, grandparents, and great-grandparents. But remember, Black Millennials are not as mainstream as some may think.

Most Black families are and have always been close-knit, with grandparents having an active role in caring for their grandchildren.

Understanding the era of the Black Millennial's grandparents—the Baby Boomers—gives you a glimpse into the life of a youngster who sat at the kitchen table, listening to stories of what life was like for their grandmothers and grandfathers. At a young age, white American neighbors and police officers accosted them during peaceful protests and sit-ins. Their great-grandfather lived through Jim Crow. Their grandfather lived through segregation, and their grandmother braved the desegregation of schools and public offices—indeed, a world they can hardly imagine.

To learn at a young age that their loved one couldn't vote, use specific restrooms, or go to certain schools certainly leaves an impression. Similarly, understanding the era of Black Millennials' grandparents or Gen Xers' great-grandparents also provides insight.

Many of their parents were the direct recipients of laws and legislation produced due to the Civil Rights Movement. Many were the first generation of Black Americans who, while still limited by broken American systems, were the first college graduates in their family line. They were the first to purchase homes without redlining and blatant discrimination based on skin color; they enrolled in vocational, post-secondary colleges and universities and received more formal and degreed education than their parents and grandparents. As a result, they occupied more jobs in corporate America and as business owners.

The makeup of the average Black Millennial lies somewhere between two interesting generational paradigms: the oppression of their known antecedents and the coming of age economic emergence of their parents' generation. They hold with them first-hand accounts of their grandparent's fight for civil rights and the newfound educational, professional, and socioeconomic opportunities their parents seized in pursuit of the American Dream. All of it translates into a group of young Black Americans who are resolute, hard-working, and who deftly repurpose cultural voids where opportunity should be to build their American Dream within that chasm.

The average Black Millennial can more readily navigate the world outside of their culture. At first glance, this shrewd adaptability appears to be a group of minority citizens who are the most integrated into mainstream society. They navigate and even thrive in the mainstream and multicultural worlds. But that doesn't mean they're integrally part of those worlds and cultures. Their multifarious nature is the most compelling fact about this go-to segment.

Uplifting Black Values, Black Life, and Black Interests

Mainstream news outlets largely ignored the death of Trayvon Martin until Black social media spheres pushed the narrative to make national headlines. Millennials made that happen, the same way Millennials and Gen Zers together pushed to make the deaths of Ahmaud Arbery, Breonna Taylor and George Floyd matter enough to broadcast on national news. Police and government officials were cavalier about investigating and working to bring justice for those Black families. Black Millennials founded socio-political organizations like Black Lives Matter, Dream Defenders and later the Real Justice Pac as a response to push for accountability. Many organizations, brands, social movements and companies that sprung up following the Zimmerman verdict, were centered around uplifting Black values, Black life, and Black interests. These young people went beyond politics and social justice. Over the next ten years, they founded social structures that would serve their community—everything from news, entertainment, education, business and technology, to goods, products, services, food, health and wellness through the Black lens; all areas whereby they felt ignored, underserved and excluded.

For the first time since their parents' early years, around the late 1960s and 1970s, during the Black Power, Black Liberation Movement, a message that revered Black lives as valuable was at the front and center of social justice, politics, race and culture.

The Black Youth Mindset Continuum:
Black Millennials and Gen Zers Living Parallel Lifestyles

When we examine the mindset of today's Black youth, we already know that differences exist between them and mainstream youth, but we've learned that differences exist also among young Black individuals. I created the Black Millennial and Gen Z Mindset Continuum to illustrate a spectrum of characteristics to help business leaders, brands and society understand these differences in a meaningful way. The three main posts on the continuum are Black youth who are Acculturated on one end, Nonconformists on the other end and Adaptables at the center. Individuals can fall anywhere on the continuum in between these posts, and they can even identify with more than one.

•————————————————•————————————————•

Acculturated   Adaptables   Nonconformists

The Acculturated

As a society, Black Americans do not tend to be considered "acculturated" as the term is generally reserved for immigrants or Americans who speak a different language instead of or in addition to English. Many Black parents who grew up in inner-city neighborhoods made the decision to migrate their families to suburban areas, and within predominantly white neighborhoods. Generally, their reasons for moving into a new neighborhood, often areas that are a step above the social class in which they grew up, is to provide their children with exposure to better education and a safer environment. Relocating away from where their parents grew up, likely removes these transplants from having close, meaningful relationships with family and friends, and it typically places them where few other Black kids live.

They're a small student body population at school, if not the only student of color. The same for their extracurricular activities and even after-school jobs—they'll often find themselves as "the only Black" in their peer group. **Their closest friends are mostly white, and their cultural exposure is more mainstream.** It's a different Black experience for them. Traditional Black culture, on the other hand, however, feels like culture shock for these kids.

The characteristics of the predominately white suburban environ-ment influence their entire adolescence. They're living in a duality of personal and social identity. For example, while they may be comfortable with their immediate family, gatherings like family reunions may be tough for them. They don't speak AAVE, (African American Vernacular English), and their extended family or other Black groups may question their "proper" speech and Blackness. Because their exposure to Black culture is limited, they lack awareness and involvement in major Black cultural affairs. Black Acculturated youth, specifically Millennials more than Gen Zers, believe they can't relate to the collective culture because they don't understand how the cultural issues that impact Black people impact them, too.

Acculturated Pain Point
Acculturated Black people are accused of "acting white" which is a hurtful misunderstanding of their background and identity.

Nonconformists

On the opposite end of the continuum are the Nonconformists. I see them as two groups: Those who embrace Black pride, enjoy Black culture and work toward Black progress. Others are angry and apathetic about Black issues. The latter are less likely to vote and are often stuck in a cycle of bitterness and pain about the downside of Black community conditions. Unfortunately, it's the behavior of the negative nonconform-ists that society tends to associate with all Black youth.

Collectively these two nonconformist groups commonly live in urban areas and if they reside in suburban neighborhoods, it's only an address. They differ from the Acculturated in that whether they live in or out of the city, they learn, work, worship and socialize almost exclusively with other Black people. **Their closest friends are Black, and they're most likely to carry the Unapologetically Black banner for the culture.**

They're anything but plain. Nonconformists are stylish, early adapt-ers, and their image and mannerisms are likely how marketers view all Black people: from ghetto to fabulous. It's important to note that some

Gen X Nonconformists would call themselves "ghetto fabulous" as a term of pride, (see more about Ghetto Fabulous in Chapter 8), however some Millennials and Gen Zers consider the term stereotypical and derogatory. Nonconformists are vociferous, opinionated and trendsetting mavericks in pop culture, slang, music, and fashion.

Nonconformist Pain Point
Because they don't conform to what mainstream considers sophisticated, they're usually stereotyped as uneducated thugs and welfare queens. This is a humiliating belief based on biased preconceptions and ignorance.

Adaptables

In the middle of the continuum are the Adaptables. They tend to possess a little of both extremes having some acculturated and some nonconformist characteristics, but they're generally more open-minded than the other ends of the spectrum. They're more exposed and worldly. They move coherently between mainstream and Black cultures. **Although they have friends who aren't Black, the majority of their closest friends tend to be Black.** Adaptables are the group of Black youth who lead many of the grassroots and crossover-brand movements. They're more likely to travel internationally, they, too, are early adapters and often try to push the envelope and live outside limiting factors.

Adaptables Pain Point
Feel the need to hold their own, while reaching on both sides of the aisle to bring the acculturated and non-conformists along.

When we share this continuum with Black youth, several say they and their peers migrate from the Acculturated or Nonconformist ends of the spectrum to the Adaptable middle post. As we learn more about them, it seems that those on the extreme ends of the spectrum grow out of those posts as they mature and become independent adults. Rarely do they migrate from Adaptable middle, to the other mindsets.

Note
1. ViaCom and BET Study on Black Gen Zers, Oct. 2020

11

Black Women: Fighters for the Cultural Good

Black women are the matriarchs holding their communities together. As observed by Toni Morrison in her documentary, *The Pieces I Am*: By all accounts Black men were the face and subject of the Civil Rights movement; Black women have been in the shadows of social and civil justice, including being a not-so-central part of the Women's Suffrage Movement. Yet, for decades Black women have been on the front lines fighting for equality—in the schools of their children, in support of their partners, in the churches and the community.

The contributions of Black women and their struggle for value and equality can be defined in several areas.

Let me explain . . .

Her Fight for Equality Has Been Consistent.

Black women influence political affairs in their communities and cities. They turn out at higher rates than other women in Presidential elections. In 2008, Obama would not have won the White House without their support; in 2008, 83 percent vs. 73 percent of other women supported Obama, and in 2012, 55 percent vs. 53 percent other women voted for him.[1] And they were crucial to Biden's presidential campaign and win in 2020; about 90 percent of Black women voted for Joe Biden over Donald Trump, making them the Democrats' most loyal bloc. For the past five presidential cycles they have shown up to the polls at higher rates than any other group.[2]

Black Women Face Unique Challenges

A Black woman's life differs from that of her white mainstream counterpart in that she is forced to be strong and resilient. For Black women living in America, being strong has never been an option. Based on societal and familial pressures, she believes she must show up with a smile to be helpful, resourceful and available. She must also "represent" to make the whole proud, be it her family or the entire Black race. She's done it in order to survive society's misperceptions of her, even though this amount of responsibility has cost her time, health, wealth and freedom.

"We are often misunderstood for wanting to be the Black man. We don't want to be the man. We like who we are, and we want the man. We don't want to "wear the pants." But because we are left with the bag, we have to do it all. So we are often misunderstood as if we choose that. We are the single parent. We want to make money . . . we want to be the ones who graduated from college. That's what we have to do to succeed . . ."

—Gen X Black woman, Atlanta, Georgia

Black Women Holding It Down

At 24.3 million strong, over half (52%) of the adult Black American population is female and account for 14 percent of all women.[3]

Black women hold the most degrees of any group of gender and skin color relative to the size of their population—and they also have the most college enrollees. Between 2009 and 2012, the proportion of Black women enrolled in college in the U.S. increased at the highest rate (9.7%), compared to Asian women (8.7%), white women (7.1%) and white men (6.1%).[4]

Black women are the conduit for reaching the total Black population.

They are drivers of the $1.6 billion total in Black spending power.

Black single moms believe they are not supported or encouraged by society to succeed.

Black women are more likely to be single moms (71% vs. 50% white moms). When compared with their white counterparts, Black single moms are often perceived as "welfare queens" and absent, uninvolved moms in general. This perception invites unwelcome criticism and prejudice, and to counteract it, a Black single mom needs to find and cultivate her own positive reinforcement.

Society's perceptions of Black women are significantly negative, when compared with society's perceptions of white women:

WHITE WOMEN	–	BLACK WOMEN
Spunky	–	Angry
Flamboyant	–	Loud
Smart	–	Uppity
Ambitious	–	Aggressive
Successful	–	Opportunistic

She feels the need to constantly validate her identity.

The angry Black woman label isn't what it used to be. Once a phrase that Black women shunned and were ashamed to be associated with, today's Unapologetically-Black mindset is likely the catalyst that has encouraged many Black women to re-think and even embrace the label. Black women wanted to be perceived as friendly, attractive and polite. But "WOKE" socially conscious commentary challenges those traits as being part of respectability politics; the notion that worthiness should be evaluated and compared with the standards of the majority. Today, showing passion, which some would call anger, is a sign of strength and liberation from "acting right." Passionate discourse and anger have motivated Black women to change their lives from undesirable conditions to worthy ones.

This new mindset has impacted Black women personally and for the betterment of the Black community. Thus, Black women are resolute upon realizing that their anger does not define them as vexed and resentful individuals. They believe it is simply an expression, and that expression is justified. Brittney Cooper writes about the revelation of Black women's "anger" in her book, *Eloquent Rage: A Black Feminist Discovers Her Superpower:*

> "Black women have the right to be mad as hell. We have been dreaming of freedom and carving out spaces for liberation since we arrived on these shores. There is no other group, save Indigenous women, that knows and understands more fully the soul of the American body politic than Black women, whose reproductive and social labor have made the world what it is. This is not mere propaganda. Black women know what it means to love ourselves in a world that hates us."[5]

Typically, a Black woman feels judged and denied access and opportunities if she is 100-percent authentic and qualified, especially in the workplace.

A Black woman wants to show up fully and authentically as she is. While the world doesn't have to embrace her appearance, she doesn't want to be singled out and ostracized for it. There have been recent conversations about the origins of the rules of professionalism. Where did these rules come from and who are the gatekeepers of professional conduct, appearance, and standards? Is the idea of professionalism rooted in racism and privilege?

Black women know that their hair, body, fashion, beauty and lifestyle choices often come into question, before their actual professional qualifications, and their ability to perform a job or be a leader.

> "Being a Black woman in America means to me that I am still having those conversations in 2022 that I had in the 80s and 90s and I can't shy away from them. Those conversations are that we have value, we are beautiful, that we are strong and vulnerable as women, and that it's not wrong to be a strong Black woman."
>
> —*Boomer Black woman, Chicago, Illinois*

Justice Ketanji Brown Jackson

Ketanji Brown Jackson is the first Black female Associate Justice of the Supreme Court of the United States in the court's 232-year history. She is the most experienced trial court judge to join the Supreme Court. Her additional pristine qualifications include service on the United States District Court for the District of Columbia for nearly eight years, giving her more trial court experience than any sitting Supreme Court justice and more than any justice since Edward Sanford, who was nominated to the Supreme Court in 1923.

She is the second sitting justice to serve at all three levels of the federal judiciary. Her colleague, Justice Sonia Sotomayor, has also served as a District judge, Circuit judge and Supreme Court justice. Justice Jackson brings more years of experience as a judge than four of the sitting justices combined. Her more than eight years of experience as a judge exceeds the combined experience of Justices Thomas, Roberts, Kagan, and Barrett when they were confirmed. She is the first public defender to become a Supreme Court justice in the history of the court, and the first justice with substantial criminal defense experience since Thurgood Marshall retired in 1991.

Bipartisan Support and Praise

Jackson was confirmed by the Senate on a bipartisan basis three times. In 2021, Jackson was confirmed to the United States Circuit Court for the District of Columbia with the support of Republican Senators. Murkowski, Collins, and Graham.

She also drew accolades from the former Republican Speaker of the House Paul Ryan: "My praise for Ketanji's intellect, character, and integrity—it is unequivocal;" and similarly from Senator John Cornyn (R-TX): "Very impressive background . . . extensive trial court experience."

Republican-appointed judge Thomas Griffith, who also supported Jackson's elevation to the D.C. Circuit after observing her work as a judge, recently said: "Her academic record is remarkable. She has a breadth of experience, which is really quite unique."

Tough questioning was to be expected during Judge Jackson's 2022 confirmation hearings. Yet, her illustrious career had no impact on the Republican senators from the 22-member committee who taxed Judge Jackson with inexcusable and unrelated questions. For example, she was asked about her LSAT scores, how she would define a woman, critical race theory, and the most ridiculous: "Do you think we should catch and imprison more or fewer murderers?" This type of questioning is not only a demonstration of disrespect, it is a disregard for the value that this brilliant Black woman brings to the justice system.[6]

Her Tribe Is Her Pride

Sisterhood is not exclusive to Black women. Yet it takes on an elevated meaning for them because they share similar challenges and celebrate one another in ways only Black women can celebrate other Black women. And that type of sisterhood runs deep. Non-Black women can be close to Black women, but rarely will they fully understand the struggles of a Black woman.

> "So, there are some things, as a Black woman, that I don't have to share with my Black girlfriends. I can just come to them and . . . whew . . . this happened and that happened. I don't have to give the backstory and bring them up to speed. They know what it is . . ."
>
> —*Gen X Black woman, Charlotte, North Carolina*

Some brands are long-term supporters of Black sisterhood and have stepped up to celebrate them. Here are a few well-known examples:

Essence Music Festival: Known as "the party with a purpose," this event is an annual music festival that started in 1995 as a one-time event to celebrate the 25th anniversary of Essence, a magazine aimed primarily towards Black American women. It became the largest African American culture and music event in the United States.

Sisters from AARP: This website and free weekly newsletter created specifically for Gen X and Boomer Black women offers fashion, health, career, and relationship advice in a fun, relatable voice that speaks to them.

Black Enterprise, Sisters Inc. Podcast: This podcast is 100-percent-dedicated to Black women entrepreneurs.

BET Her: An extension of the BET brand, BET HER is the first network designed to broadcast content that is Black-women centric.

I like the new sisterhood supporters, too, like Urban Spinster. This digital platform, created by Sadia Sanders, speaks to primarily single, never-married Black women over 40. Sanders is a thoughtful, articulate, host, yet has no problem interjecting her no-nonsense and sometimes raw presentation of various topics—from dating a narcissist, to home buying strategies—while dispelling societal myths and redefining the word "spinster."

When brands and companies strategize to include positive, relatable, aspiring messages for Black women, they win!

Notes

1. *Black Girl Magic: The Power of Black Women in Elections,* aflcio.org, 2016
2. "How Black women worked to secure Joe Biden's election as president," Megan Botel, usatoday.com, 12/2/20
3. African American Women: Our Science, Her Magic, neilsen.com, Sept. 2017
4. DiversityJobs.com
5. *Eloquent Rage: A Black Feminist Discovers Her Superpower,* Brittney Cooper, St. Martin Press, 2018
6. "Judge Ketanji Brown Jackson Is One of the Most Qualified Nominees for the Supreme Court," demandjustice.org, 2/25/2022

12

Black Men: The Path Forgers

Defining a Road Forward While Overcoming Stereotypes

Millions of good Black men are doing the right thing: working hard, being good fathers, making positive contributions to society, etc. They are becoming more visible role models and building new foundations for themselves, their family, and the Black community.

For example, Black fathers continue to defy the stereotype of absentee dads. Most Black fathers are there for their children—as much as or more than White fathers. According to the National Center for Health and Statistics, 70 percent of Black fathers who live with their children are more involved in their daily lives than 60 percent of white fathers.

Many young Black fathers understand the importance of a father being present, responsible, and supportive caretakers.

Claudette Roper, an artist and adjunct Professor at Columbia College in Chicago, wrote the following poem, "The Fathering Kind," as a tribute to and validation of the many Black fathers that we see and know in our community. She wrote this poem in celebration of Father's Day 2022 and read it aloud to a group celebrating Juneteenth, which was the same weekend.

The Fathering Kind[1]

The fathering kind . . .

steps in, steps up and shows out in spite of the lack of bloodlines. Coaching the coach-less, speaking life into those burdened by life's limits.

Modeling comebacks, even as the world revokes opportunity
    after opportunity.

The fathering kind . . .

Rejects the dismal crafting of oppression cultivated in heavy rotation.
    Indoctrination embraced—by even some of our own sun-kissed
    brethren—tilling seeds of mistrust, misrepresentation, and hyped-up
    laments of the missing.

The fathering kind . . .

Wiping butts, tears, noses, combing hair, tying ties, dancing, shaving.
    Delicate conversations, noteworthy first steps, dates, graduation,
    jobs, heartbreak.

Daddy, Pops, Popi, Uncle, Cousin, Brother, Grandad, Bebop.
    They are here in the physical. They are here with the spiritual.

The fathering kind . . .

Providers, protectors, professors against the odds. Curse you out,
    lift you up, streetwise, book smart, quiet storm, tavern hanging,
    old school playing, silky smooth.

Encouraging nod of the head, deep sigh of concern, glance of approval—
    the look of love.

The fathering kind . . .

Answers to callings beyond self. Patriarchs must cover everyone!

Balling, que-ing, church going, grass cutting, household repairing,
    driving—lessons demonstrating how to maneuver and live life fully
    with purpose.

The fathering kind . . . Defying insidious imagery

deflecting from the reality of who and whose they are. And yet, they
    know who and whose they really are!

The fathering kind . . .

Guttural laughing, smack talking, work going, truth speaking,
    bear hugging, caresses of endearment.

Armed with words of wisdom, comfort, courage, compassion,
    encouragement."

Friends, enforcers, organizers, confidants, and lovers standing in the void.
    The fathering kind . . .

For the brothers that do—even when they get it wrong—we relish the day. Grateful, grace-filled memories of those no longer in this realm.

Celebrating with those who are here, in this space at this sacred time. We honor, we adore, we support, WE LOVE YOU—the fathering kind!

In addition to embracing fatherhood, the *Black Men Making It in America* report by the American Enterprise Institute (AEI), shares two important "good news" findings about Black men:

- First, the share of Black men in poverty has fallen from 41 percent in 1960, to 18 percent in 2018.

- More importantly, the share of Black men in the middle or upper class—as measured by their family income—has risen from 38 percent in 1960, to 57 percent in 2018.[2]

The report identified three factors associated with this success that have enabled Black men to achieve middle and upper-middle class status: education, work, and stable relationships. I have discovered two additional factors that can be attributed to their success: the Black Church and the military.

Education provides Black men with the opportunity to find employment that provides a steady income, and healthcare benefits.

Stable relationships offer improved longevity, wealth, health, happiness, and companionship in place of loneliness and isolation.

Black Church: In addition to religious and spiritual growth, the Black Church, compared to non-Black Church organizations, is a culturally nurturing and nourishing place for Black men. The Black Church is a safe haven for Black culture, history and community. It encourages Black men to lead with pride, and dignity within its four walls, and in all aspects of their lives. The Black Church offers generations of support and accountability, and importantly, there is recognition and respect for Black men.

The Military: The military often helps Black men find purpose, teaches discipline and perseverance, provides an opportunity to learn new skills, and helps pay for college.

I am a big fan of the late August Wilson and his work. He was a masterful playwright who wrote ten epic stage-plays from different decades during the 20th century. His work centered around Black life in America. He won a Pulitzer Prize for two of his productions, *Fences* and *The Piano Lesson*. I've had the opportunity to see several of these plays at the Goodman Theater in Chicago, and for anyone who has had the same chance, I'm willing to bet their lives were all the better because of it.

Wilson explores Black identity and Black struggle. He wanted to help Black America understand themselves. What I love about Wilson's writing is how he tells the Black story, the Black experience, and our truth, particularly from the lens of Black men. He tends to showcase more Black men than women in his plays and very few, if any, whites.

In addition, the playwright presents the full range, balancing depictions of Black men as we know them: confident, heads of households, bringing-the-check-home-to-mamma proud; entrepreneurs, flawed, stubborn, introspective, vulnerable, community and church leaders, firm in their convictions, stand-up men, brave, lovers of Black women, and more.

While fans and critics praise Wilson for the impact his work has had on the theater community and society, few, if any, acknowledge the Black man's perspective as a quality of Wilson's storytelling.

The Mission to Overcome Black Male Stereotyping

Black men are wrought with judgments and stereotypes in America. Whenever Black men are brought up in conversation, a reaction seems to make people noticeably uncomfortable and defensive. In America, Black men are synonymous with drugs, violence, sexually predisposed, unemployed, and impoverished.

Additionally, according to a report about Black men mentioned in an article from *The Guardian:*

". . . their athletic prowess, physical stature and affinity for entertainment, especially musical entertainment, are inordinately sensationalized in this country. A successful Black man is almost exclusively portrayed as a music mogul or sports star, and when that is the singular depiction of success, it implies limited choices for everyday boys and young men who aspire to be something in America."[3]

The general public substantiates negative perceptions of Black men by pointing to their imprisonment rate as they are more likely to be imprisoned versus whites or Hispanics. Yet, statistics on Black men's imprisonment rate is only data. Those numbers rarely include why there is a disproportionate population of Black American men in prison, that is until *The New Jim Crow* was published.

Ten years ago, Michelle Alexander, a lawyer and civil-rights advocate, published *The New Jim Crow: Mass Incarceration in the Age of Color-blindness*. The book considers not only the enormity and cruelty of the American prison system but also, as Alexander writes: "The way the war on drugs and the justice system has been used as a 'system of control' that shatters the lives of millions of Americans, particularly young Black and Hispanic men."

Alexander puts the justice system on trial by revealing how a significant percentage of the African American community is warehoused in prisons or trapped in a parallel social universe. They are denied fundamental civil and human rights, including the right to vote; the right to serve on juries; and the right to be free of legal discrimination in employment, housing, access to education, and public benefits.

Alexander's work has brought nationwide attention to the broken justice system and has encouraged many concerned citizens and organizations to galvanize against mass incarceration.

Years before the release of *The New Jim Crow*, imprisonment rates were already on the decline, and the book's release, along with its widespread support, helped contribute to even more of a decline. According to the most recent statistics from the Bureau of Justice and the Pew Research Center, the nation's imprisonment rate is at its lowest level in over two decades. The most significant decline has come from Black

Americans, whose imprisonment rate has decreased by 34 percent since 2006.[4]

More than Century of Stereotyping

In the early 1900s, the Confederate South organized racial smear campaigns targeting Black people. Over the years, the media and Hollywood fueled stereotypes and exaggerated negative perceptions about them.

Although today, there are more positive images of Black people in the media and movies, Black men are still more likely than any other group to be attached to negative and exaggerated portrayals in films and media.

The practices from the past have contributed to unfavorable perceptions and lasting impressions about the Black community, especially Black men who are perceived as criminals and sinister monsters who must be stopped from tainting and wreaking havoc on American society. As a result, Black men are presented as the most vilified group of people in the media. In contrast, Hollywood and the media tend to showcase balanced depictions of white male images and characters, especially heroes.

I enjoy watching dramas and action-packed movies, and television-series for entertainment and escapism. More often than not, the lead characters are white and male. They are the heroes who save the girl, the town, and the world. I watched the Marvel characters who are portrayed with extraordinary strength like Superman, Spiderman, and Captain America; the most physically fit, and quick learners like James Bond, Jason Bourne, and John Wick. These characters get shot, fall ten feet from some elevation, roll, get up and still kick the butts of six assailants. And let us not forget the old-school heroes: The Lone Ranger, Tarzan, the animated character Popeye and more! Don't get me wrong, I enjoyed these characters. They were entertaining. Yet, in the absence of Black (or any other ethnic heroes), the Black community would often refer to them as *Super White Boys*. There was an apparent damaging message to both Black and white audiences: the presumptive belief of who is supposed to be on top and who is not.

No wonder *The Black Panther* movie (2018) meant so much to Black Americans who were overjoyed upon its release. I saw it three times on the big screen.

In addition to its historic box office success ($1.3 billion), the portrayal of a powerful, respected Black male character, combined with a Black cast in front of and behind the scenes, was a groundbreaking celebration of Black culture.

In an interview with *The New York Times,* Camille Friend, who oversaw the various hair designs, encapsulated the Black community's readiness for such a moment and said this: "We're in a moment when people are feeling empowered about being Black."[5]

Reframing How We Measure the Black Man's Impact on the Black Community
A Case for Reframing How Black Men Are Perceived

Positive Realism in marketing and advertising is a marketing tool that flips negative stereotypes on their head. It provides a chance for everyday, progressive, hard-working, enterprising, and educated Black Americans to be seen as normal, respectable people. It allows us to be human, fun-loving girlfriends, romantic boyfriends, admirable father figures, and easy-going mothers.

In this section, we're studying the fabric of the Black family arc: Black men, Black women, and Black youth. In creating this arc, my goal is to underscore the integrity of my claim that Black consumers are valuable and essential not only to the marketplace but to decision-makers who want to forge a positive alliance and win the loyalty of this consumer segment. I'm setting the stage for why Black people should be in the spotlight and in so doing, debunking the longstanding, baseless, negative stereotypes that have plagued an entire race for nearly one-half of a millennium.

Starting here, I want to tactfully demonstrate Positive Realism on the subject of Black men in America. Why? Well, straight and to the point: comparatively, the stats don't look good for Black men. They never really have. While, as a researcher, it is of utmost importance to tell the truth—to let the data speak and support the findings. There's another side of the coin that I would like to explore regarding Black men.

During my many months of research for writing this book, it was relatively easy to pull positive statistics and general data on Black youth and Black women. But it was challenging to get the data I needed to illustrate who the Black man is and how he shows up in our families, society, community, and America. Sure, I could find plenty of numbers to support how problematic he is. I could quickly download the statistics demonstrating Black men's role in a crime or their absence from their families and households. But data that show their accomplishments in education, the workforce, and their family and community contributions? Scarce.

I want to pose a bold question: Are we, as researchers, marketers, and storytellers, asking the right questions when we survey Black respondents about Black men, their makeup, their accomplishments, and their impact? Asking the right questions, and even scrutinizing those questions to ensure accuracy and relevance, is paramount to a researcher's duties. There are traditional methods to carry out market studies. Every seasoned researcher knows the basics: outlining the objectives and details about the target; how the research will be used; creating the methodology; outlining the timing and investment. The research tools—screeners, discussion guides, and survey instruments—must include questions that are worded and presented in a way that does not imply bias to the respondent. This is the way we do our work. Is that way begging to be reexamined?

Black Men Do Not Live Parallel Lifestyles to White Mainstream Males

In a general census, questions are generated using a standard rubric of assumptions or criteria considered to be normalized social activities, assets and behaviors. For example, historical census questions would seek to confirm the household makeup: a husband, wife, children, and other inhabitants. There wasn't a checkbox for two husbands, two wives, or a domestic partnership made up of one wife and one non-binary individual. Today there is. So then, could it be reasonable to surmise that how we seek to gather data about Black Americans, but particularly Black men, is biased?

When we seek to understand, for example, what gainful employment a Black man engages in, is it in a typical nine-to-five, blue- or white-collared context? Do we even ask about the various ways in which they contribute to their community that may not be typical to that of a white male?

When we seek to poll Black respondents, what questions are we asking and why? Black men do not live parallel lifestyles to mainstream white males; their day-to-day does not look the same as that of their white American male counterparts.

If the data to be gathered are set by a researcher or client who only understands or who only has reference to the typical criteria that make up a mainstream white male's lifestyle, then it's probable that the data, when asking the same criteria-set questions to a Black man, would likely not result favorably.

Here's an anecdotal case in point. The average middle-class white American male lives in a neighborhood made up of predominantly white residents, that has a grocery store or market within one mile of his house, and whether he lives with his wife and children, or he is separated, the children generally have access to one parental or family member being available after school, or he or his partner have the financial means to keep their child in an after-school program. And this white male contributes to his community by coaching the little league football team and annually going on an international trip to a developing country to dig water wells.

The average middle-class Black American male lives in a neighborhood of predominantly Black residents, where the nearest grocery store is three miles away. Additionally, there is a shelter near his home, where a sizeable homeless population gathers daily for a place to sleep, but the food isn't always available. He lives at home with his wife and two children. He and his wife both work. He owns an auto-mechanic shop, and she works at a bank. They get by, but can't afford to eat out often and take family vacations or after-school care.

From my experience, that Black man (and his wife and other family members) will in all likelihood, start an organization or partner with his church, or other men in his community and circle, to create an after-school sports program or a meal-serving program.

When I see—when we see—the frequent and rampant data that indicate the lack of presence of Black men in positive aspects, we all do this internal head scratch, confused about how it is these studies are constantly reporting the same findings. Even I am guilty of thinking at one time, "well, the numbers don't lie." And while the numbers can be accurate regarding the data that are being reported, the question really becomes, what questions, exactly, are being asked? As a researcher, one must ask:

- What is being examined? And in what method— with what set of leads?
- Where are you looking?
- What does all of this mean?

My point is to shout from the rooftops: BLACK MEN SHOW UP! They're here! They're present.

I am posing these questions and proposing the reexamination of how research is conducted for Black respondents, because from my experience as a Black woman, and the experiences of friends who are Black, and especially from my experience as a researcher, finding positive statistics for Black men for this book shouldn't have been that difficult.

Yes, Black men make up a disproportionately large population of the prison systems in America. Yes, a higher proportion of Black men are absent from the household of their former partners and some of their children's lives, compared to other races. But in contrast, there are Black men who are not in prison, on drugs or involved in deviant behavior. Instead, they're living a progressive, commendable lifestyle, be it single or with a partner.

There are Black men who, because they chose not to attend college, attended a vocational training school where they learned to cut hair, repair mechanics, carpentry, plumbing, culinary arts or real estate. There's a significant population of Black men in the military. And I can tell you: they don't all work for a large corporation or a small business.

Many Black men start their own businesses. Many of them organize, lead and participate in sports-league competitions in their own communities—initiated by them or perhaps their church—which may not be recognized as a formal state-registered organization. Many have founder's and director's roles in non-profit organizations that provide food, clothing, shelter or beneficial and recreational programs that help advance and improve their communities.

You'll find droves of these stand-up men in local churches. The younger ones are on Instagram and YouTube cooking at home, giving relationship advice to women and men, recording comedic TikTok tips about caring for a newborn, combing their daughters' hair, traveling with other like-minded friends, or working out with their significant other.

Mainstream looks primarily at the places white males show up, and just because Black men aren't there, too, doesn't mean they aren't showing up at all. It means they aren't showing up where you're looking. But we know that they're here, where we're looking.

Black Men Showing Up and Making an Impact

I called the Black Youth "The Forerunners," and I called Black women "Fighters for the Cultural Good." And I purposefully deemed Black men "The Path Forgers" because today, and historically, they have always had to forge their own paths. They have always had to be creative about how they earn a living and how they take care of their families. Not only in today's statistics, but even as far back as sixty years ago when colleges desegregated in the South, Black women have always been more college-bound than Black men. Black men as heads of households summoned their sons to forego college and work a trade to provide for the family. Today the number of Black male enrollments lags behind Black female enrollments, even at HBCUs. There are several reasons, including the number one obstacle, access to financial resources. Thank goodness for optimal leaders and role models (like Robert Smith, the Black billionaire mentioned earlier, who paid off the student loan debt for the entire 2019 graduating class for the Black male Morehouse College) and Black-conscious authors, scholars, and professors like Dr. Cornel West, Gelani Cobbs, Ta-Nehisi Coates, and Colson Whitehead.

But I call Black men The Path Forgers today, because now more than ever, Black men are not only showing up. We see them. The data are starting to illustrate their mainstream impact with more businesses registered, fewer incarcerations, and more positive family-related findings. I admire the fight of this resilient segment; I admire what they're doing to show the world that they are not who they've been portrayed and, too often, perceived to be.

The Path Forgers

I have a colleague whose father, Steve Childress, Jr., is an architect and general contractor in Memphis, Tennessee. A licensed contractor can work on small projects under five-thousand square feet but for anything larger, an engineer must be involved. Her father didn't go to school to be an engineer. Still, he worked with his hands and was the first Black student to attend a previously segregated high school in North Memphis, the same school where he also enrolled in a vocational program learning the carpentry trade. Later, he obtained his contractor license, and for thirty years, he has been a small-business general contractor, designing and constructing commercial properties for over two hundred businesses in Tennessee. If you looked him up in an architect's directory or searched articles in an architect's digest, you wouldn't find his name. But the community knows him. He had a hand in building out the interiors of some of Memphis' most iconic shops and restaurants from Beale Street to the outskirts of Memphis' suburbs. He couldn't afford to go to college because of both cost and time. He raised five children and was a Little League football coach. He's an example of how everyday Black men in America make a living, raise their families and contribute to their communities through unconventional, often under-recognized programs.

Victor James, Sr. and Artistic Motions Raise the Bar for the Chicago Style Steppin' and Culture

(Hint: It's about Love of the Dance and Love for Black People)

I love to step. Steppin' is one of my favorite pastimes; we do a lot of it here in Chicago. Chicago Style Steppin' is a stylized swing dance that originated more than 60 years ago. Back in the day, it was known as the Bop (different from the flamboyant Philly Bop) that quickly spread from Chicago to Detroit. Over the years, dancers evolved the dance to several variations of style. At some point in the nineties, steppin' became more structured to 3-beat, six or 8-count format, and a new style known as "new school" steppin' was created. The new format requires a commitment to learning the foundational count (until mind and muscle memory kick in), the moves, footwork, and lane management. It's a beautiful dance and a big deal in Black culture. In several major cities in America, one can step somewhere every day.

As the new style flourished in Chicago, steppers with higher levels of mastery and proficiency—most of them Black men—began traveling across the country, teaching others eager to learn and master various techniques in the dance. Currently, Chicago Style Steppin' is one of the few urban dance styles performed predominantly by Blacks, age 45 and over, in several major metropolitan cities—from Detroit to Baton Rouge and New York to Los Angeles!

The dance has also become popular with many Millennials, creating a resurgence in couples' dancing.

Often referred to as the "Black Fred Astaire," Victor James, Sr., a nationally known and well-respected dancer in the steppin' community, fell in love with steppin' and began teaching it in 2003. You can see his passion for dance in the way he dances and by listening to portions of his story:

> "I was a somewhat introverted guy who found a way to relate to others through dancing. I've been moving my body to music since I was about six years old and will probably dance until I leave this earth.

> "The first time I saw Chicago Style Steppin', I immediately fell in love with it. I fell in love with every aspect of the dance, the culture, the clothes, the music, all of it.

> "Since my introduction to the dance, I've managed to find my way and establish my style in the dance."

Victor sees the "holistic" benefits of the dance (i.e., exercise, a confidence builder, etc.) and how others can grow in the dance. That's why he created Artistic Motions, a national digital platform of accessible, engaging, comprehensive content, including a cache of more than forty free instructional videos, YouTube dance video content, photos, and words of encouragement, to help others. He has expanded Chicago Steppin' in ways that others haven't.

Today, Victor has nearly 4,000 online students and has attracted close to three million viewers to his dance content on YouTube and Facebook platforms. His stated goal: "To spread the love and joy of the dance while emphasizing and adhering to a standard of excellence."

> "I want people to fall in love with the dance as I did. I want to inspire people to learn this dance—to feel good emotionally and physically. I'm trying to get people to see and feel what I feel! It's a holistic experience. I'm trying to give Chicago Steppin' the positive representative platform I think it deserves."

Like any other dance community composed of people, the steppin' community is not without its challenges. It is ego and male-driven.

Big egos are the brash element of the culture that can be competitive and cliquish. Some of the better dancers are sometimes condescending to those new to the dance or perceived as not up to par with their standards. Thus, steppin' dance instruction is often perceived as "a hustle" in some communities. Victor James is one of a few instructors to whom the hustler mindset can't be attributed. He is laser-focused on his mission of owning the "smooth and elegant space" in Chicago Steppin'. He most likely owns that particular dance space as he maintains his own lane and his own style of the dance.

Victor has an MBA and more than twenty years of professional corporate experience but leaves his ego at the door when providing instruction and interacting with others. Instead, he brings confidence, style, and humility to the dance floor and shares this mindset with his team and students.

The Artistic Motions team consists of primarily professional Black women, including his wife, business, and dance partner, Lisa Jeff James, a licensed mechanical engineer.

Victor consistently showers his team with accolades and respect and welcomes newcomers to the dance enthusiastically and patiently. It's no wonder that he is the only Chicago Style Stepper' (with a partner) featured in the National Museum of African American History and Culture at the Smithsonian in Washington, D.C. He has made Artistic Motions a quality brand while being a stand-up man.

In 2022, he hosted the second Artistic Motions Major Weekend Event (AMMWE) in Houston, Texas. I was one of over 300 steppers in attendance from all over the United States. I was blown away. The event was more than a party. It was a three-day professionally executed high-level cultural experience (and a sponsor's dream). It's common to hear Victor say, "I just want to love on my people." And he delivered on that desire through AMMWE. The event was a love fest of camaraderie, steppin', good music, and good food.

Attendees enjoyed a costume ball, steppers' workshops, a smooth Jazz and R&B Saturday day set, a blue-jean brunch, and the weekend highlight, a Saturday night black-tie gala. Black folks love to get dressed up, and as we say, "Everyone was 'fly' all weekend!"

In my excitement, I began doing my "research thing" and conducted some informal interviews with the guests. "Proud" was the word that surfaced most from attendees when asked about their experience. Guests weren't surprised at the quality of AMMWE, but they felt validated by a Black man and his team who delivered a class-act event.

Contrary to the constant barrage of bad news about our community Black Americans are not allowing this information to define them. We know and see the many "Victor Jameses" and "Steve Childresses" in our community who are breaking stereotypes and leading the Black community to higher ground. Society and brands should heed, recognize and engage more with these good Black men. They are everywhere and they mean everything to the Black community.

Organizations that Support and Celebrate Black Men as We Know Them

There are millions of Black men in America, and the world, who are being themselves and consciously doing their everyday "good guy" thing. For their more than 281K followers, creators of the popular Facebook page, *Good Black Men,* share posts, videos, and stories that acknowledge and validate good Black men. We see the story of an 18-year-old high school graduate who was, at one time, homeless yet finished at the top of his class and won a full ride to Harvard; and the soccer star who has earned $10.2 million, yet chooses to help people from his community over updating his damaged iPhone or purchasing a Ferrari. There are messages of encouragement, truth statements, and moments to celebrate unsung heroes.

Here are a few more organizations where Black men have a positive presence in the community:

Real Men Cook

Since 1990, Real Men Charities, Inc., has presented Real Men Cook® as a way to improve perceptions of Black men relative to their families and communities. This annual all-day celebration is held on Father's

Day to recognize "real men," the Black men we know, respect, and love—locally and globally. Real Men Cook is the largest, longest-running, and most-anticipated Father's Day celebration of its kind. It was conceived and launched in Chicago by entrepreneurs Yvette Moyo and Kofi Moyo as a local Father's Day family celebration. The baton was passed to son, Rael Jackson, who has been leading and managing the organization for more than three years.

Today, Real Men Cook is the leading urban Father's Day experience. It's a food-tasting, family celebration, featuring men volunteering to cook for and serve the community. Ticket-sale proceeds are shared through partnerships with non-profit organizations. Cooking is an example of what Black men are willing to do for their families and communities, giving up Father's Day pampering to make a difference. Said one participant:

> "I enjoy Real Men Cook because of the camaraderie. There's a great group of men and women supporters always there to help to influence and give you ideas and recipes, etc., and it's nice to know that somebody else is cooking beside you. So the money, the time, it's all well worth it, and we know that we are doing it for a charitable organization as well."

Fathers and father figures don chef's hats and cook for the community. The original concept grew to be celebrated in as many as 13 cities and has evolved into a national Father's Day tradition. Among the high-profile men who have participated in Real Men Cook is former President Barack Obama, who referred to the annual event as his "family tradition."[6]

National Pan-Hellenic Council (Fraternities)

Since the early 1900s African Americans have sought out independence and freedom. When they got the chance to create something of their own, it was a breath of fresh air for many to become involved with fraternities and sororities. The values of these organizations are all about education, service, merit, and brotherhood. Many men look at fraternities as life-saving organizations and a way to uplift and push them to the heights of their abilities.

100 Black Men of America

The organization 100 Black Men of America, Inc., is recognized as the nation's top African American led mentoring association. Their mission is to improve the quality of life within Black communities and enhance educational and economic opportunities for all Black Americans. There are more than a hundred 100 Black Men chapters delivering unique programs that address specific needs in local communities. Since 1963, they have provided a proven blueprint for mentoring and developing young people into future leaders by surrounding them with a positive network and giving them opportunities that they may not have thought were possible. They stress the importance of being successful and making a difference—stressing the importance of obtaining and applying education, and providing them the tools that empower them to be self-sufficient, cultivated, civic and business leaders.

THE OPPORTUNITY

We are seeing more diverse images of Black men in the media, post George Floyd. Some are benign characters clearly swapped for white characters; many are stereotypes; and a few are the images of Black men that we know—strong, caring and involved caretakers, family men, great best friends, and boyfriends who are straight and gay. Still, most of the positive images of Black men are underrepresented.

Featuring Black men in positive realistic situations, and telling stories that rarely get told, is like a magnet to the eyes, ears and hearts of the Black community. It helps to reframe society's overarching perceptions of them, and provides a sense of value in a world in which they are experiencing a disproportionate amount of social injustice.

✖

Changing the Narrative

August Wilson Wrote Plays That Provide
Balanced Depictions of Black Men [7]

Jitney (1979) Conflicts between generations and different concepts of loyalty and identity, (circa 1970s).

Ma Rainey's Black Bottom (1982) Racism in history of Black musicians and white producers, (circa 1920s).

Fences (1984) A man in his fifties, once a gifted athlete, works as a garbage man now, and how his bitterness affects his loving wife and son, (circa 1950s).

Joe Turner's Come and Gone (1984) Former slave examines racism and discrimination, (circa 1910s).

The Piano Lesson (1986) Brother and sister have different points of view about keeping or selling an heirloom with carved depictions of family members and their history, (circa 1930s).

Two Trains Running (1990) A restaurant owner worries what will happen when the city comes to claim the building through eminent domain. A young activist tries to organize protests and rallies that can help save the restaurant, but the restaurant owner is not so supportive. A community on the brink of change, (circa 1960s).

Seven Guitars (1995) Blues singer is newly freed from prison when he's asked to sign a record deal after a song he recorded months before becomes a surprise hit. He struggles to right wrongs. Black manhood is also a theme of the play, (circa 1940s).

King Hedley (1991) King Hedley, a man whose self-worth is built on self-delusion, shows the shadows of the past reaching into the present as King seeks retribution for a lie perpetrated by his mother regarding the identity of his father, (circa 1980s).

Gem of the Ocean (2003) The story of the first generation of African Americans to emerge after the end of the Civil War. A man choosing to "die innocent rather than live guilty" sets off a chain of escalating events, (circa 1900s).

Radio Golf (2005) This play concluded Wilson's Century Cycle and is the last play he completed before his death. A successful entrepreneur aspires to become the city's first Black mayor. This bittersweet drama of assimilation and alienation traces the forces of change on a neighborhood and its people caught between history and the twenty-first century, (circa 1990s).

Notes

1. "The Fathering Kind," © Claudette Roper, 2022

2. "Black Men Are Succeeding in America," cnn.com, 7/3/2018

3. "When the Media Misrepresents Black Men, the Effects Are Felt in the Real World," Leigh Donaldson, theguardian.com, 8/12/2015

4. "Black Men Making It in America," Brand Wilcox, Wendy Wang and Ronald Mincy of the American Enterprise Institute (AEI), www.aei.org, 2018

5. "*Black Panther* is a gorgeous, groundbreaking celebration of Black culture," Tre Johnson, vox.com, 2/23/2018

6. Realmencharities.org

7. Source: PBS.org and breakingcharacter.org

13

Black Immigrants:
Foreigners Only by Name

While African Americans are Black by race, not all Black people in the U.S. are African Americans. This statement, mentioned earlier in "Black, African American, POC or BIPOC?" (*see page 50*) is worth repeating here because to understand Black America, is to understand foreign-born Black people fully.

A Black immigrant is defined as any person born outside the United States to non-U.S. citizen parents and who identifies as Black or African American alone or in combination with another race or races in the American Community Survey (ACS).[1]

Black immigrants' and U.S. born Black Americans' sun-kissed mela-nin-rich skin often causes American business leaders to think of them as identical. Black immigrants are better-educated, higher-income earners, and more likely to be serial entrepreneurs, when compared to the U.S. population. Long and short, they have contributed significantly to the overall population growth and the economic value of Black America. Yet, when business leaders think about multicultural marketing or "immi-gration," Black immigrants are rarely, if at all, on their radar.

Major Players in the U.S. Economy

A Pew Research study finds that immigrants now account for about one in ten Black persons in the United States. That 10-percent figure is up from 3 percent in 1980.[2] Further, in 2018 alone, Black immigrant households earned $133.6 billion, paid $36.0 billion in taxes ($22.8 billion in federal income tax and $13.2 billion in state and local taxes), and had a spending power of $97.6 billion. This is a significant contribution to the overall Black spending power.

Black immigrants are particularly active in the healthcare industry, especially as nurses, personal-care aides, and nursing assistants. Almost 3 in 10 (27.5 percent) of all Black immigrant workers—or more than 750,000—work in the healthcare sector.

Among all immigrants, Black immigrants have the highest rates of English language proficiency. More than 90 percent of Black immigrants speak English well or only speak English, compared to nearly 60 percent of Hispanic immigrants and about 81 percent of Asian immigrants.

Overall educational attainment is equal to the U.S. population, yet almost 40 percent of African immigrants have at least a bachelor's degree and nearly 16 percent have advanced degrees. Thus, African immigrants are more likely to hold a master's, professional, or doctoral level degree than the U.S. born population.[3] Many Black immigrants also operate small family-based businesses. Part of their success is due to the entrepreneurial skills they developed in their home countries.

While Black immigrants want to become Americans, they are also determined to maintain their home country's culture, traditions, and beliefs. The practices from these traditions have caused a domino effect of influence on Black and mainstream cultures. First-generation immigrants have been vigilant about preparing and passing down recipes that not only show up in their kitchens but have also fueled successful Black immigrant-owned and operated restaurants across the country (and globally).

Many Dominican women, primarily, are credited for their work with hair braiding, hair straightening, and kinky/curly hairstyles—straight and natural—all worn by Black women. The use of herbs to create centuries-old concoctions for "whatever ails you," also originated in the homelands of these immigrants, were undoubtedly passed to Black Americans, and then adopted by the mainstream into a multimillion-dollar industry.

From a lifestyle perspective, Black immigrants are very focused and goal-oriented. Given that many in their homelands are struggling in poverty they tend to place a value on educational attainment, entrepreneurship, investments, and they have created and supported media from their respective cultures. Nonetheless, none of these practices have prevented Black immigrants from experiencing the wrath of anti-Black racial prejudice in addition to anti-immigrant discrimination.

The Tension Between Black Immigrants and Black Americans

The majority of Black immigrants entered the country more recently than 1980, well after the Civil Rights Movement. Thus, many have not understood how slavery has impacted the U.S.-born Black American lens, how the Black American fight for equality is ongoing, and how this ongoing struggle has benefited their presence in this country. Many adopt mainstream's perceptions about U.S.-born Black Americans and therefore distance themselves from U.S.-born Black people. Clusters of Black immigrants typically live together in mixed or predominantly white neighborhoods. This does not mean that they dislike Black Americans. They want to keep their cultural identity intact while maintaining their standards and status as over-achievers and contributors to their respective cultures.

Recognition of their homeland, culture and contributions to the Black American community, and the U.S. economy is a means of showing respect and appreciation to this growing and influential segment of the U.S. population.

Black Immigrant Population by Region of Birth, 2018[4]

Country of Birth	Number of Black Immigrants	Share of All Black Immigrants
Jamaica	694,208	16.3%
Haiti	667,943	15.6%
Nigeria	369,740	8.7%
Ethiopia	276,897	6.5%
Ghana	195,710	4.6%
146 Other Countries	2,059,521	48.3%
Total 2018	4,264,019	

United States Population of Black Immigrants[5]

Estimated total 2022	4,600,000
Projected total 2060	9,500,000

Notes

1. Black immigrant definition: boundlessresearch.com
2. "A Rise in Black Immigrant Population Changes Understanding of Black America," npr.org, 2/17/22
3. "Power of the Purse: The Contributions of Black Immigrants in the United States," newamericaneconomy.org, 3/19/2020
4. *Ibid.*
5. boundlessresearch.com

14

BLACK LGBTQ+ Individuals:
The Fairness Fighters

Blasts of pride, pain, fashion, glamor, and a profound presence of friendship, community, and family were the impetus for the television series POSE. Critics say POSE changed contemporary popular culture because it highlighted the origins, allure, celebration and popularity of ballroom culture during the late seventies and eighties by Black gay, trans and drag pioneers. The series helped create awareness of this genre and it put Black and Latino trans actors on the map.

After watching the series, I took away sentiments that were universal, regardless of sexual orientation or lifestyle: the fact that we all experience challenges and triumphs, love and loss. Those themes permeated each episode and endeared me more to the LGBTQ+ community, as it is clear: we're all human, and we're all in this human experience together. I was especially drawn to the storylines where the characters, mostly Black and Latino, had to fight for their lives; for fair and equal treatment, for acceptance in the world. While fictional, I've observed and researched these realities finding them to be real, for real people, in real life.

LGBTQ+ STATS

- 11.3 million LGBTQ+ adults live in the U.S.
- About 40 percent of LGBTQ+ adults are people of color, including 12 percent or an estimated 1.2 million U.S. adults who self-identify as Black and LGBTQ+[1]

Black LGBTQ+ Lives Matter

I've never spoken or written these words in this way until now. I feel it's necessary to distinguish that while the Black Lives Matter message encompasses all Black people, saying Black LGBTQ+ lives matter is significant because it speaks to an additional layer of challenges, situations and responsibilities associated with the Black LGBTQ+ experience. Here are three facts to consider:

Black LGBTQ+ individuals face the compound effects of multiple forms of discrimination for being Black and LGBTQ+

The launch of the LGBTQ+ Movement in 1969, following the Stonewall Riots, was the door opener for promoting Gay Rights issues. Today, gay rights is a critical political and social issue. Younger generations are increasingly identifying as LGBTQ+ in the U.S. They tend to be much more likely, than older Americans to embrace ideas of themselves as something other than heterosexual. At the same time, the gay community continues to fight through their own fear and the judgment, hate, and fear of others to which they are subjected, along with discrimination. A foundational challenge of the LGBTQ+ community is society's perceptions of them as "appalling sinners." First thoughts about the LGBTQ+ community is that they are overly sexually active, pedophiles, and rapists. Black LGBTQ+ people are prone to heightened versions of these negative perceptions and therefore live and endure an even more difficult experience.

> "In our community, the Black Church, with all its influence, continues to marginalize gay people. Also, you can't talk about Trans lives and Black Lives Matter together. Black Lives Matter is perceived as more important than the other."
>
> —Reginald Osborne, senior strategist and business leader in Multicultural Marketing

Another reason for the added burden on Black LGBTQ+ individuals is that generations of historical prejudice against Black Americans, in general, have overshadowed the unique issues of the Black LGBTQ+ community. Even now, America has yet to fully understand how the intersection of Black and LGBTQ+ has led to discriminatory practices in the workplace, in hospitals and doctor's offices, and when interacting with religious institutions and law enforcement. These have resulted in more significant economic and healthcare difficulties for this segment. An analysis of some of the data from the 2020 Center for American Progress[2] will help to explain:

The year 2021 was one of the deadliest years in history for violence against Black transgender individuals, at least 16 of whom had been killed in hate incidents as of April 2021.

Twenty-five percent of Black LGBTQ+ individuals report experiencing discrimination when interacting with law enforcement; 13 percent of white LGBTQ+ respondents said the same.

Seventy-eight percent of Black LGBTQ+ individuals report that discrimination has affected their likelihood of being hired or their employment opportunities; 55 percent of white LGBTQ+ respondents said the same.

Fifty-six percent of Black LGBTQ+ individuals report that discrimination has affected their ability to retain employment to some degree; 46 percent of white LGBTQ+ respondents said the same.

Fifty-five percent of Black LGBTQ+ individuals report that discrimination has negatively affected their ability to rent or buy a home to some degree; 32 percent of white LGBTQ+ respondents said the same.

Eighty-three percent of Black LGBTQ+ individuals report that discrimination has negatively affected their physical well-being to some degree; 61 percent of white respondents said the same.

Black sexual minority men are also more likely than their white counterparts to experience discrimination within LGBTQ+ spaces. They reported the highest racial/ethnic stigma levels in LGBTQ+ spaces. White sexual minority men reported the lowest levels, with Asian and Hispanic/Latino men falling in between.[3]

Nonetheless, the Black LGBTQ+ response has been to organize, become activists and empower themselves.

It's a tremendous uphill battle for all LGBTQ+ people seeking equality. "Coming out" in American society is no joke. As LGBTQ+ individuals come out, they must also prepare to steel themselves from criticism, ostracizing, judgment, discrimination, and much more. For Black LGBTQ+ people, it's double-duty. Black Americans are often perceived as having less value than others and judged more harshly. Black LGBTQ+ people face these challenges with amplified voices to educate America and global audiences about their value as Black Americans and the unapologetically Black LGBTQ+ culture. Consequently, Black LGBTQ+ support organizations are exploding nationwide, assisting in social advocacy, health and wellness, workplace conditions, and more. While many reference "Black" in their title, their mission often encompasses broader groups of persons of color. Here are a few examples:

Native Son is an intergenerational movement, community, and platform created to inspire and empower Black gay/queer men. No other organization globally supports this community with an emphasis on wellness, empowerment, and amplification.

Black Gay Weddings spread shared photos of Black Gay love and marriages across Instagram and TikTok social media platforms. Their tagline: "Elevating the love of LGBTQIA+ BIPOC & Interracial Couples." The images of the couples are beautiful, and several of the wedding scenes are presented in luxury and are simply spectacular.

Black & Pink National is a prison abolitionist organization dedicated to abolishing the criminal punishment system and liberating LGBTQIA2S+ people and (Lesbian, Gay, Bisexual, Transgender, Queer and Questioning, Intersex, Asexual, Two-Spirit,) people living with HIV/AIDS. They are affected by that system through advocacy, support, and organizing. Black & Pink National, founded in 2005, now has a strong grassroots network of 11 volunteer-led chapters and more than 20,000 current and formerly incarcerated LGBTQIAS2+ and people living with HIV/AIDS (PLWHA) members located across the country.

National Black Justice Coalition (NBJC) is a civil rights organization is dedicated to empowering Black LGBTQ+ and same-gender-loving (SGL) people, including those living with HIV/AIDS. As America's leading national Black LGBTQ/SGL civil rights organization focused on federal public policy, NBJC has accepted the charge to lead Black families in strengthening the bonds and bridging the gaps between the movements for racial justice and LGBTQ/SGL equality.

Trans Women of Color Collective uses art, healing, and comprehensive support to protect and lift trans women of color who have been disenfranchised or victimized by violence.

Zuna Institute is a national advocacy organization for Black lesbians created to address the needs of Black lesbians in health, public policy, economic development, and education.

Black LGBTQ+ people are a force as cultural shapeshifters in Black, U.S., and global cultures.

"Every single element of what we know of as Pride and gay rights and, especially, the pre-Stonewall homophile movement, was borrowed from the Black Freedom Movement."

—Eric Cervini, LGBTQ+ historian

Long before Stonewall Riots, there Was the Black Freedom Movement.

The Black Freedom Movement originated in the urban and Upper South. Activists organized massive demonstrations to achieve desegregation of public facilities, better housing and job opportunities for Blacks, and eliminating discriminatory governmental policies.[4]

Gay activists were present during the Black Freedom Movement. Fighting for civil rights was a fight for gay rights. The prolific and prophetic writer James Baldwin wrote profound essays about the Black Freedom Movement. Bayard Rustin, a close advisor to Dr. Martin Luther King, Jr., was one of the most influential and effective organizers of the Civil Rights Movement. He was also the organizer of the March on Washington for Jobs and Freedom March on Washington, where 250,000 people gathered at the Lincoln Memorial in 1963.[5]

There are many other Black gay activists like Baldwin and Rustin who, back in the day, began protesting for gay rights. For example, there were sip-ins (much like the sit-ins) at bars and restaurants that refused to serve Blacks and gays.

Thus, began the influence of early gay rights activists who took their cues from the foundation prepared by Black activists—and Black-gay activists who get little credit for their contributions.

A New Generation Continues to Effect Change and Acceptance

Modern-day influence includes activism for awareness (Black LGBTQ+ struggles), inclusion, and acceptance, but also to put-on-blast cultural acculturation.

Let me explain . . .

RuPaul, TV Personality, Drag Queen, Model, and Actress, Is Credited with Bringing LGBTQ+ Culture into the Mainstream.

RuPaul is the host of RuPaul's Drag Race, a reality TV show where RuPaul and judges search for "America's Next Drag Superstar." Although the show's shtick is the presentation of lip-synced performances, fabulously over-the-top fashions, hair, and make-up, the show also helps both the contestants and the viewers understand how to love themselves more. This is also why the show has become such a celebrated part of television.

RuPaul's avid promotion of self-love has helped launch the careers of more than 120 drag queens. He was also the first face of M.A.C. Cosmetics (1994), which likely helped inspire makeup use for straight and gay Black men. In fact, several queer beauty bloggers—Black and white—speak to everyday users in layman's terms. Tarek Ali is a Black and gay beauty vlogger who features products for dark skin and Black features. As of this writing, Tarek has 329K followers.

RuPaul has also helped raise money for AIDS epidemic awareness. The fund has raised more than $400 million to date.[6]

House Music is Black Queer Music!

The recognition that House Music *is* Black queer music is the perfect nod to house music's origin and ownership. For decades, many believed House Music was created by mainstream and adapted by Black culture. But it's the other way around.[7]

House music has a distinctive psychedelic beat created in Chicago by DJ Frankie Knuckles in the late 1970s or early 1980s. It was in the Warehouse, a venue attended exclusively by Black and Brown LGBTQ+ men, where Knuckles introduced this music, not referenced as House back then. This venue and other gay nightclubs provided a safe space for these men who were constantly harassed in most public places.

As the music spread to broader groups of the gay community internationally, subcultures emerged. In 1988 the subgenre called acid house catalyzed a British youth culture explosion when dancers discovered that the music's psychedelic bass lines acted synergistically with the illegal drug ecstasy (MDMA, or 3, 4-methylenedioxymethamphetamine, a hallucinogen and stimulant),[8] and mainstream began adapting house music as its own. House music has made a huge comeback, with Beyoncé and Drake course-correcting the perception of its origin by using the music and re-mixing the music in their songs. Other musicians and entertainers will follow their lead.

Ballroom Culture Creates an Expanded Definition of Family for the LGBTQ+ Culture

The Ballroom Scene (also known as the Ballroom community, Ballroom culture, or just Ballroom) is an African American and Latino underground LGBTQ+ subculture that originated in New York City. The Balls are competitions between individuals, groups, and "houses" of drag queens who perform different categories like vogueing or catwalking. While Ball events gain attention for their ornate and colorful fashions and pageantry, it's the kinship system of "houses" that undergirds the true value of the Ball culture.

The "houses" are chosen families with anointed "mothers" and "fathers" who guide and support their "children." They are an uplifted collective, rejected by both white supremacy and Black homophobia. Alongside the Black Freedom Movement, Ballroom soon spread across the U.S., continuing to confront systems of oppression and demanding more freedoms.

On numerous occasions, I have lent an ear to several painful stories about Black trans and queer young people who were forced out of their family homes. Ballroom is a non-judgmental, safe space that helps the LGBTQ+ community find family, resources, and themselves. Through the Black and Latino experience, Ballroom helps instill pride in the LGBTQ+ communities.

Notes

1. UCLA School of Law, Williams Institute, January 2021

2. Black LGBTQ+ individuals Experience Levels of Discrimination, American Progress.org, https://www.americanprogress.org/article/black-lgbtq-individuals-experience-heightened-levels-discrimination/

3. "Multiple Minority Stress and LGBTQ+ Community Resilience among Sexual Minority Men," Elizabeth A. McConnell, Patrick Janulis, Gregory Phillips II, Roky Truong, and Michelle Birkett, *Psychology of Sexual Orientation and Gender Diversity,* vol 5(1), Mar. 2018, 1–12, National Library of Medicine

4. Stanford University–Southern Culture

5. *The March on Washington:* history.com

6. "RuPaul Charles: Creating Opportunities for the LGBTQ+ Community," McKensie Commings, *Black EOE Journal,* July 2018

7. "House Music is Back. Let's Remember It's Roots," Lynee Denise, harpersbazaar.com, 6/30/2022

8. *House Music:* Britannica

15

Undeniable Black Influence: Redefining Cultural Norms

Black APRR—
Authentic **P**ositive **R**elevant **R**epresentation

Over the decades, I've watched catchphrases saturate the market in an attempt to communicate the industry's commitment to embracing various emerging consumer markets. Many industry endeavors, culturally speaking, were full in policy, but flat in practicality. That's because people are at the center of fulfilling these commitments or simply checking a box that says they did it. How can one determine if affirmative action; multicultural marketing agendas; or Diversity, Equity, and Inclusion commitments are truly inclusive? Internal to my market research practices, over the years, I have been using Black APRR—Black Authenticity, Positivity, Relevancy, and Representation—as a way to encourage brands to consider the Black lens when developing strategies and messages for this audience. I was delighted to learn that I am in alignment with Marc Pritchard, Procter & Gamble's chief brand officer, who wrote about the "Three R's"—Representation, Relevance, Resonance in a blog post on P&G's website and shared their value and insights at the 2021 ANA Multicultural Conference.

When I am asked to review marketing strategies that target Black consumers, or when a national multicultural campaign comes across my desk, I can immediately recognize its potential as to whether or not it will be valuable and resonate with Black consumers because it either possesses or lacks Black Authenticity, Positivity, Relevancy and Representation.

The value and significance of incorporating Black APRR in a brand strategy or marketing campaign is key to winning the loyalty of Black consumers. Black APRR focuses on celebrating differences instead of ignoring them. And it demonstrates trustworthiness because it includes truthful components that resonate with Black buyers.

When leaders want to win the trust and loyalty of Black consumers, they must start by asking: Is it Authentic? Is it Positive? Is It Relevant? Is there Representation?

Black APRR is quite difficult to fake. Decision makers should not simply swap out the photo in print material and place it in a store or swap out talent in a commercial, having them dress in the same wardrobe and read the same lines. It's not effective.

So, what are Black consumers requesting? They want to see and feel the authenticity in the campaign, product, or service.

- They need to know and feel that (targeted) messages are really for them and not just their money.

- They want to be shown as culturally relative, positive, and not based on negative, outdated stereotypes.

- And they want to be represented the right way—in advertising and the media and to know who is behind the messaging.

Cultural Shapeshifters, especially the young ones, are like Black APRR zealots. They're enthusiasts especially for seeing themselves authentically. Trends, gimmicks, and politically correct slogans will not overshadow real Black APRR with this group. They immediately sense Authenticity, or the lack thereof, when reading a social media post or discovering a new line of products in their local big-box store. And many of them, in positions of great influence, are quick to call out the presence or absence of Positivity and Representation. They also want to know who was at the table and who was behind the creation of products clearly designed for, and marketed to Black buyers. In fact, 86 percent of Black

Millennials say that, to win their endorsement, a brand must possess values that align with their own.

A Snapshot of Highly Influential Black Contemporaries and Their Undeniable Influence

This $1.6 trillion spending-power consumer group demonstrates hard work and resourcefulness. There's value in their dollars, but also value in Black culture and their presence. Yet, when we examine Black representation in almost every consumer category, Black ownership, leadership, and inclusion have been sorely lacking. Highly Influential Cultural Shapeshifters are redefining American culture in two ways:

> **First:** They are juxtaposing a "by Black for Black" stand against mainstream America that has historically underrepresented and misrepresented the Black consumer yet monopolized the Black dollar.

> **And Second:** They are leading the culture and marketing space with Black insights. They naturally and organically draw on the Black lens and the Black experience with insights and to educate and create opportunities for the whole.

Here are some examples of Undeniable Influentials who have launched crossover movements and have been among the most visible:

> **Rihanna**   Born in 1988, this singer, actress and businesswoman, launched The Fenty Beauty® makeup line in Sephora with 40 shades of makeup colors, so that a broad range of women, including those of darker hues, can be reached and provided with colors and products appropriate for their particular skin color and skin type. Maybelline, L'Oréal, and Lancôme had 40+ colors in their coffers but never used this approach when they marketed to women. Their cultural norm was to speak to mainstream women—women of lighter skin tones. Following the Fenty launch, these brands followed suit and they increased their customer base.

Robert Smith   The Black businessman and billionaire paid student loans for every 2019 Morehouse College graduate. Morehouse is an HBCU (Historically Black College/University). Smith's efforts re-ignited the national conversation about the rising cost of college and the long-term impact of student loans and have contributed mightily to a student loan forgiveness movement.

Anya Dillard   Some might call her an over-achiever, but by age 20 this young woman had already become known for her work as an activist, philanthropist, performing artist, entrepreneur, content creator, and aspiring filmmaker. She is also the founder of The Next Gen Come Up, a non-profit organization that encourages young people to participate in activism and community service. Dillard also uses her art and others to increase awareness about activism and motivate them to organize through media and creativity. As quoted in verygoodlight.com, Anya said this about the power of Blackness:

> "Our Blackness is a diamond that has been dragged through the mud, mountains, lava, and rain and has yet to show a single scratch; our Blackness is resilient and deserves to be honored for its power and uniqueness. As big of a social construct as race is, our Blackness is what unites us. It connects our experiences, our fears, our traumas. We all have a different 'Black experience,' but alas, it is all a part of one interconnected Black experience."

Kendrick Lamar   Born in Compton, California, in 1987 and known for his progressive and socially conscious song writing, Kendrick Lamar is often cited as one of the most influential rappers of his generation. I'm not squeamish about profanity. My parents, who are both deceased, did not curse but if they were alive today, they probably would die if they heard some of the chatter I have had with my close friends. Yet, the first time I heard Lamar's music, I cringed. Then I focused on his messages and stories. His rawness helped illuminate the realities of life in underserved and disenfranchised communities. He speaks from the Black culture lens about the struggles in the 'hood and includes messages of resilience and positivity. The authenticity and relevance of his message are relatable to several groups of people worldwide, especially the Hip-Hop community.

His ability to connect deeply with millions won him 14 Grammys and the 2018 Pulitzer Prize for his 2017 album *DAMN*. Awarded by Columbia University in New York, the Pulitzer often acknowledges individuals in education, communication, science, journalism, and music—but never before for Hip-Hop music. The offering of the prestigious Pulitzer to Lamar is a demonstration of respect and is a big deal for the Hip-Hop music industry and the Black community. Chuck Arnold of the *New York Post* further keenly and simply summarizes the impact of Lamar's Pulitzer win in an article he wrote early in 2022: "It is a reflection of the times and social change that needed happen."[1]

Byron Allen   Born in 1961, Bryon Allen is the founder, chairman, and chief executive officer of The Allen Media Group (AMG). Those aware of Allen most likely know of him as a comedian, producer, and host of the comedic talk show, *Comics Unleashed*. What many don't know is that Allen is a media mogul who owns one of the largest cable network portfolios in the industry. AMG owns ten 24-hour HD television networks including: The Weather Channel, comedy.tv, cars.tv, es.tv, justicecentral.tv, mydestination.tv, pets.tv, recipe.tv, local now, and The Weather Channel en Español.

AMG also owns The Grio, an American television network and website with news, opinion, entertainment, and video content geared toward Black Americans. When launched in 2020, The Grio.TV projections included reaching over 100 million U.S.

households via over-the-air broadcast television stations, cable/ telco/satellite platforms, and free digital streaming.

Another Black media platform under AMG's umbrella is HBCU GO—the leading media provider for the nation's 107 Historically Black Colleges and Universities. HBCU GO offers viewers the best in live sports, original series, documentaries, films, comedy, and edutainment programming produced by leading African American producers, directors, and students from select HBCUs.

Allen has created an awareness about the opportunities for Black-owned media platforms, and other media platforms that serve the Black community.

For example, Joseph Sanchez is one who answered "the calling." Sanchez is the owner and CEO of SWAAGTV a 24/7 local news and entertainment, broadcast, cable, and streaming television station. SWAAGTV (Shows With African American Greatness) is Chicago's first and only 24/7 local Black broadcast and streaming television station presenting news and entertainment that serves Chicago's local Black communities, including households without cable. It was created by Mr. Sanhchez to serve the 1.7 million African American population that represents 600,000 television households in Chicago. According to Mr. Sanchez, "SWAAGTV is where Black Chicago is seen and is heard."

Tyler Perry This American comedian, filmmaker, and playwright, born in New Orleans in 1969, has parlayed the $150 million he predominately made from his work featuring the Black "Invisible Middle"—working class community—into Tyler Perry Studios. Based in Atlanta, TPS is home to all TPS productions and is the venue where *The Black Panther* was filmed in part. Perry was able to effectively tap into this Invisible Middle group that many marketers ignored or refused to acknowledge. He created TV programs and movies for the big screen that feature a predominantly Black cast, but he has also garnered a large mainstream audience for his productions.

Issa Rae   Born in 1985, this author of the Awkward Black Girl blog, which then became the HBO TV five-year show *Insecure*, reportedly inked a $40 million deal with WarnerMedia (HBO, HBO Max, Warner Bros TV, and Warner Bros feature films first-look). Like Tyler Perry, mentioned above, and Oprah Winfrey with her OWN network, they are providing unprecedented opportunities for overlooked Black actors and Black behind-the-camera production crews.

Nikole Hannah Jones   Born in 1976, this American investigative journalist and staff writer for *The New York Times* founded the 1619 Project (and wrote the book) to commemorate the 400th anniversary of the beginning of American slavery. It aims to reframe the country's history by placing the consequences of slavery and the contributions of Black Americans at the very center of our national narrative. The 1619 Project book was on *The New York Times* best-seller list for 13 weeks.

Misty Copeland   Born in Kansas City in 1982, this talented Black American ballerina became the first Black principal dancer of American Ballet Theater; rejected for years by the Ballet industry for being too dark and having a different body type than traditional ballet dancers. Copeland has inspired hundreds of girls who look like her and who are built like her to join ballet. Copeland works tirelessly today to ensure that underserved women have an opportunity to perform for live audiences.

Stacey Abrams   As a former Georgia State Representative, author, politician, and lawyer, Abrams used her influence and leadership to help register 800,000 voters in Georgia—an historically "red" state. The voter turnout from her efforts turned the state "blue," which ultimately helped elect Joseph Biden the 46th President of the United States. Her efforts likely contributed to the 2021 election victory of Raphael Warnock who became the first Black Democrat elected to the Senate in a Southern state; this consequential run-off election flipped control of the Senate from Republican to Democratic leadership.

Beyoncé   At age 36, Beyoncé became the first Black woman to headline Coachella Valley Music and Arts Festival in California. Her April 2018 billing broke historic records for the festival, and she used her popularity and the Coachella opportunity to share the Historically Black Colleges and Universities (HBCU) Homecoming experience with the world. She also filmed the entire experience— from backstage to performance—and created a documentary (*Homecoming*) which contributed rich (Black) content that first aired on Netflix in April 2019.

Jason Reynolds   The best-selling author, imaginer, and storyteller you may have never heard of sold 6 million books between 2014 and 2022. Born in 1983, he writes about two Black children, for all children, to encourage readers (who are not exclusively Black) to embrace their story—the stories that don't exist. Says Reynolds, "I put the kibosh on uncomfortable conversations that kids are trying to have."

Dwayne Wade   Founded in 2014, Wade Cellars has separated itself from the crowd as an authentic producer of approachable California wines and a principled advocate for the wine industry. Established as a partnership between former basketball star, style icon, serial entrepreneur, philanthropist, and social activist, Dwyane Wade and the Pahlmeyer family, Wade Cellars strives to make the wine industry more inclusive to people of all backgrounds by consciously growing production and creating opportunities for access and education to all those who choose to indulge in this affordable luxury. Wade is also the author of *The New York Times* best-seller, *A Father First: How My Life Became Bigger than Basketball*.

These Cultural Shapeshifters represent only a handful of hundreds of Black influencers who are teaching business leaders and society about the importance of leading with Black insights. Black cultural insights can also lead to engagement opportunities in the mainstream. When you get it right with Black Americans, you get it right with the mainstream.

Note

1. "Why Kendrick Lamar is the greatest rapper of his generation," Chuck Arnold, *The New York Post*, 5/13/2022

PART FOUR

Rethinking Black

How Our Mainstays Outshine Stereotypes in
Relationships, Community, and Representation

Rethink Black Relationships:
Replacing the Myths with Meaningful Truths

I wanted to present sound research of the Black economic impact in America, in my previous book *Black STILL Matters in Marketing.* It was necessary and helpful to contextualize the data to connect the dots, and make the data relatable to my clients. So I used real-life, relevant stories, a step beyond simply pointing to the numbers. Clients and audiences took an interest in these stories about relationships, bits of historical facts and the inner world of Black life that they hadn't heard before. This in turn sparked conversations that were truly transformational. As these conversations and my perspective have evolved over the years, I discovered that it was not only important to help America see Black economic value. It became paramount to add dimensionality to Black people and help America to see Black intrinsic value. To ensure that my research is qualitative, and not merely numerical data, I highlight Black relationships, community, traditions and customs—a glimpse into Black perspectives, revealing who we really are. That means (yes, we're consumers, but) we're human, with challenges, triumphs, lives, communities and most importantly, relationships that influence so many aspects of our lifestyle and behavior. We're thought leaders and changemakers. It's important to take a look at how Black Americans communicate, relate, detest, protest, commune, like, love and get along with one another, as well as with others.

One thing that struck me during my research for *Black STILL Matters in Marketing,* similar to the sparse research I found in search of positive statistics for Black Men, discussed in Chapter 12, is how little research and numbers I could find on the topic of Black love, Black family and Black relationships. As a Black woman, I'm familiar with the joy and vibrancy that comes from being in community with my fellow friends and colleagues. My life, like many others, is enriched because of relationships and friendships with other Black people. I wondered if this aspect of Black life was invisible? Or is it ignored? Why can't America see Black love the way I see it?

Let me explain . . .

In the last ten years, the Black community at large has begun creating positive and uplifting content *and* speaking up about the lack of representation in the media and the marketplace. They see what I see: Black men and women in healthy, loving, committed same-sex and heterosexual relationships; Black girlfriends and Black male friends supporting one another; Black consumers supporting Black entrepreneurs and businesses; Black families growing and keeping traditions alive.

It's been over a decade since I wrote *Black STILL Matters* and since then, I have been able to gather better data that tells a different story about how Black people love and relate to one another. Not only that, I'll share some insightful experiences I've encountered that puts this new data into context.

16

Black Relationships

Black Love Exists, and It Means Everything

From its inception, Black love has been a household expression born out of the fracturing of Black love and marriage. This began during the Middle Passage, when women, such as Hagar Blackmore in 1669, recalled being "stolen away from her husband and the infant that nursed on her breast."[1]

Mainstream media constantly show Black men as criminals, deceivers, and absent fathers. The media tells us that Black women are angry and cannot keep a good man. The overarching perception is that loving Black marriages and relationships don't exist.

Recently, I was delighted to find that *The New York Times* published a series of stories based on the premise: "What is Black Love Today?"[2]

While mainstream media fails to accurately and often portray the beauty in Black love, I have observed it to be a feel-good sense of warmth and belonging for Black men, women and children. It is the intimate aspect of love, but it is so much more. Black love is a unique balance of unification, togetherness and support for three main groups within the Black experience:

- Loving partnerships, relationships and marriage
- Trusted friends and family
- Legacy-building within the Black community

These groups are an extension of who we rely on, and "do life" with.

Black Love is Different

A Black loving relationship has similarities to other relationships in terms of the desire to be committed, being a team, supporting each other, having respect, communication, etc. But Black love is also different. It runs deep and has many layers of situations that have shaped the Black community's perceptions about a couple's need to exist comfortably and affectionately in their culture. From back in the day when our ancestors had restraints and restrictions on who they would love, to the present day, Black love is scrutinized by the mainstream and the Black community on what is accurate and relevant. For example, the Black community often points to the Huxtables, from *The Cosby Show* (a TV sitcom about an upper middle class family that ran from 1984–1992), and the Obamas as the most appreciated examples of Black loving couples. TV sitcom couples, George and Louise Jefferson (*The Jeffersons* and *All in the Family*), James and Florida Evans (*Good Times*), Carl and Harriet Winslow (*Family Matters*), Gina and Martin Payne (*Martin*), Curtis and Ella Payne (*House of Payne*) and Dre and Rainbow Johnson (*Blackish*) among others, are relevant too, with conditions. The upside about these couples is their embrace of values and the cohesive family units. The Black community also perceives these couples as "funny," "real," and people they know.

The downsides are couples, characters and storylines laced with buffoonery and stereotypes. We also hear rumblings about couples "fighting too much." The affinity with the Obamas and Huxtables leaves few things for society to pick apart. There were questions about Barack Obama being Black enough[3] and a few not believing in the existence of upscale families like the Huxtables—Claire, the wife, was an attorney, and Cliff the husband an obstetrician. Yet, the Obamas and Huxtables have aspirational qualities to break negative stereotypes on a national stage, which is a paramount desire of the Black community.

Black Queer Love

As awareness and acceptance of LGBTQ+ relationships increased, so did homophobia. New and trending terminology like "grooming" (the act of befriending a child to molest them) became more undeservedly associated with the LGBTQ+ community as gay kids and teens started coming out in record numbers. Any adults—parents, teachers, therapists, clergy, etc., who supported these youth and LGBTQ+ rights were labeled "groomers."

Black queer love is often excluded in Black love conversations posing a double-whammy challenge: gay and racism. As Black people, Black gays are criticized and ostracized for not fitting into mainstream standards. Black gay and transgender men are especially frowned upon, more so than gay women, as they are accused, under the false pretense that their existence emasculates Black men. This mindset often stems from an overall lack of respect, the uninformed and those following anti-gay religious doctrines.

The good news is that more conversations about Black queer love are occurring on social media, and images of these couples are showing up in advertising, programming, and movies. A few expressions like loyal, humbling, grounded, unapologetic, authentic, and trusting are used to describe Black queer love by the Black gay community. Although these characteristics are not exclusive to the Black gay community, they are used to educate and ward off homophobic attacks.

Black Love for the Black Community is Growing.

This $1.6 trillion spending-power consumer group demonstrates hard work and resourcefulness. There's value in their dollars, but also value in their culture, and their presence. In every consumer category, however, Black ownership, leadership, and inclusion has been sorely lacking. Responding to the disparity, cultural shapeshifters are juxtaposing a "Buy

Black for Black" stand against a mainstream America that has historically misrepresented the Black consumer yet monopolized the Black dollar. As a result, a momentous modern grassroots culture has been born.

Most Black Americans understand the practice of and need to support Black-owned and operated businesses (*see Chapter 7: Blind Spot #5*). It's not racist, as some in society believe. Buying Black is Black love in action. Black companies pump wealth into the community by providing jobs and contributing to its vitality.

John and Maggie Anderson made headlines in December 2008 when they pledged to help jump-start the economy by exclusively supporting Black-owned businesses for an entire year beginning January 1, 2009. They formed The Empowerment Movement, wrote a book, *Our Black Year.* They were guests on CNN and Fox News, and articles about their buy Black proposition put the Andersons on the map then, and today in a big way. Maggie is the face of The Empowerment Movement and continues to be a sought-after speaker and resource for organizations, colleges, and universities, and the media.

The "Buy Black" grassroots movement has lasted decades and gained traction following the death of George Floyd and the Black Lives Matter protests. Buy Black websites, serving as directories of sorts, have sprung up all over the internet showcasing an array of Black businesses including dry-cleaners, florists, wineries; product manufacturers, contractors and service professionals, including CPAs, medical doctors, attorneys, and more that reveal the breadth of revenue generating opportunities (and pride).

In fact, during the summer of 2020, mentions of "Black-owned" in Yelp reviews were up 617 percent[4] compared to the same time in the previous year and the number continues to climb.

Worth? Black Love? *What about Black-on-Black crime?*

It's becoming a popular question asked by my non-Black colleagues when I share the good news about the Black community—the stories that rarely ever get told. Of course, there is white-on-white crime, Asian-on-Asian, and Hispanic-on-Hispanic. Yet, Black-on-Black crime appears to be promoted as more prevalent than others.

According to a study by the Department of Justice, the share of same-race crime for Blacks who commit crimes against each other is 62 percent, versus 57 percent of whites who commit crimes against other whites. There are more occurrences in the Black community, but not by as large percentages as many believe and would expect. Given that most Blacks live in highly populated urban areas, stories of crime and Black-on-Black crime become highly circulated. Additionally, the news media primarily promote perceptions about Black-on-Black crimes inserting race in the stories, but not in similarly reported stories with other ethnic groups (*See the discussion about destruction of Black community during protests, Chapter 3*).

From 2011 to 2020 there has been a spike in crime. The percentage of violent crime victims who were Black increased by 3.2 percent to reach a peak of 32.7 percent in 2020. By contrast, the percentage of total victims who were white steadily declined from 69.1 percent to 64.7 percent over the same period. This small increase hides a more dramatic recent trend because the percentage of Black offenders fell several percent from 2011 until 2019. That year, it jumped 1.0 percent, and in 2020 it jumped another 1.2 percent.[5]

Again, these are small percentage changes, but considering the surging crime numbers and the fact that African Americans make up a relatively small percentage of the total population, the implications are huge.

The relative share of offenders by racial groups followed a similar trend to the corresponding share of victims. While the spike in crime is hurting a lot of people, Black communities bear the heaviest burden.[6]

I'm not suggesting by any means that these stats should be ignored. Yet, over the years, stats like these and how Black America is presented in the media have bolstered society's perception that every Black community is the wild, wild west.

I've lived on the southeast side of Chicago for over 30 years. It's a working-class community of retired teachers, police officers, postal employees, etc. A number of empty nesters and two generations of single women and men live here, too. It's quiet and stable, with a park nearby where I walk my dog and run, and say "good morning" to the runners and active seniors who walk daily. We are good neighbors who maintain our properties and look out for each other. There are many stable low-crime communities like mine across the nation. But the face of crime has always been that of the Black community. There is love in the Black community, even those struggling with high crime. Black activism has inspired many neighbors to fight for increased protection and take responsibility sustained by love and community.

Rethink Black Community:
Exploring Cultural Customs and Spaces that Propel Black Connectedness, Acceptance, and Kinship

Black culture is made up of collective experiences, both historical and contemporary, embracing remnants of African identity and American identity.

Customarily, the mainstream agenda is sterilizing and presenting a homogenous front. Perhaps we'd all belong if we all adhered to the same customs, behaviors, beliefs, and living standards. But it still doesn't quite work that way. From being exposed to the ugliness of racism at a young age to over 25 years of examining behaviors of primarily Black and other consumers, one thing I can say for certain: people of color cannot erase what makes them who they are. Therefore, instead of requiring everyone else to become the same, my appeal has been to celebrate what makes us different. If a marketer or storyteller wants to understand Black American culture, it will be a historically rich, compelling, and worthy effort. One opportunity is to delve into the importance of **Community** for Black people.

Our spaces usually begin as ideas or acts that don't take up too much space or make too much noise, spaces that seem insignificant to "others."

For example, Negro Spirituals came about as a small but mighty act used by enslaved people to release sorrow and anger and fuel themselves with the strength, courage, and hope they needed to realize freedom and a future. I can imagine how enslavers back then thought the moaning and murmuring of singing slaves were meaningless. But for Black people, it was a weapon against oppression, a tool to communicate; it was therapy; it was small, but it was *something*.

Then came little religious meetings, the origins of the Black Church. And as emancipated Black people began living civil lifestyles, it was essential to create Black systems, structures, neighborhoods, and codes that catered to the Black needs and demands of Black citizens (e.g., Black Wall Street) when mainstream America simply would not.

The Black Church carried on traditions of religious beliefs but also created a culture for Black Church etiquette, how Black people sing, dance, and worship, how Black ladies wear their hats, and how Black preachers preach, (*see Black Church discussion in the next chapter*).

HBCUs, sororities, and fraternities created a culture of Black excellence in education and civil responsibilities. The NAACP created a culture of protecting Black people through the competent and ubiquitous civil and legal defense. The NAACP Image Awards gave Black entertainers and public figures a space to be formally recognized for their achievements. The launch of BET, *Ebony, Jet, Black Enterprise,* and *Essence* created a space for Black stories to be told and celebrated. And it has been so throughout the decades. Today, we have the raw realness of the syndicated radio show, *The Breakfast Club,* hosted by Charlamagne Tha God, and DJ Envy and formerly Angela Yee. It is featured in 90 markets and heard by over 4.5 million listeners each week. Blavity, the successful online platform created for Black Millennials, is doing the same.

These are a few safe spaces, safeguarded by nuances that mean one could be themselves—speaking, dressing, laughing, joking, dancing, worshiping, disciplining, learning, and living *their way.*

Communities, products, and services for Blacks have always been created to balance and meet the needs of overlooked consumers. Be in little gatherings or nationally recognized establishments—it has been a series of communities characterized by intimate togetherness—a type of togetherness that eludes mainstream influence or involvement that propelled Black people and their agenda forward. Black American culture, civil rights, and social progress have survived hundreds of years because of the Black community. Black people decide who to support, what products to buy and what places are safe based on their peers, recommendations, and community. Our history of building and keeping our community strong keeps us connected—especially today.

Let me explain further . . .

Notes

1. "2019 marked 400 years of 'forbidden Black love' in America," Diane Stewart, washingtonpost.com, 12/26/2019

2. "What is Black Love Today?" Veronica Chambers, *The New York Times,* 2/11/2022

3. *Black enough:* Acting a certain way that is uniform to common Black beliefs and behavior.

4. "Buy Black Movement Helps Black-owned Businesses" abcnews.go.com, 10/23/2020

5. "Who Suffers the Most from Crime Wave?," The Heritage Foundation, Crime and Justice, April 2022

6. *Ibid.*

17

The Black Church

Demonstrating Value through Social Justice

I grimaced when I heard the reaction of an ad agency's senior strategist to a proposed church strategy for a Black American initiative for one of their clients:

> "If I hear one more idea to use the Black Church as a resource for this initiative, I'm gonna scream!"

I understood her frustration. She wanted to ensure that the team was developing new and innovative strategies for the initiative.

To them, marketing to the Black Church is considered an "old school" or dated strategy, thus ineffective. It's logical, then, that she'd misunderstand the significance of the Black Church. Because of its importance to the Black community, anytime a brand, organization or even public figure is endorsed by the Black Church, it's endorsed by its people. Depending on the brand's offerings, products and services, the Black Church can be an important partner toward the success of any marketing initiative.

The Black Church has deeply rooted cultural relevance, reverence and trust in the Black community. It's the largest and oldest-running business in the Black community. It is also the only institution owned and controlled by members of the Black community. Because of that, its influence and grassroots reach far exceeds most media outlets and many marketing campaigns.

Understanding the Dynamics of Black Worship

Black worship is traditionally different from how white people worship. Black Americans, in their worship, want to learn something and feel something, specifically God's Spirit.[1]

It's emotional and demonstrative, especially in COGIC (Church of God in Christ), Baptist, small-mission churches, and non-denominational churches The worship environment of the Black Church is where people are their most vulnerable selves. They don't have to wear their Blackness as a thing to be appreciated or despised. They faithfully pour into the pews of their safe haven, their church, to be unburdened of all of the demands of life. They don't have to perform. They don't have to be afraid. This experience, on the literal and proverbial altar of the sanctuary, is described as "where pain and burdens are laid down." Here, Black people can hope, be happy, and heal. They can believe, affirm, and be reaffirmed that their desires in life can indeed be theirs. They can cry, they can cheer, they can shout, they can contemplate without pretense.

Black church services are orderly and spontaneous, lively and celebratory, and rooted in the teachings of Jesus Christ and his biblical promises of liberation, love, and hope.

Dr. Hermene Hartman, TV talk show host of N'DIGO Studio and editor/publisher of the now digitized *N'DIGO Megapaper*, targets Black middle- to upper-class readers in the Chicagoland area. Dr. Hartman has a testimony about the Black Church's contribution to *N'DIGO*'s success:

> "I decided to include the Black Church as a distribution point for *N'DIGO*. It was a brilliant move for N'DIGO. Many tried to discourage me from partnering with the Black Church, but when the pastor held up *N'DIGO* and encouraged the congregation to read it, it was the best PR and advertising I could ever have."

Many brands haven't had the same access to church pastors as Dr. Hartman. Brand exposure and relationship-building through the Black

Church have proven to be the "secret sauce" needed to engage the Black community.

Notably, Black churches that include social justice in their messaging and community advocacy outreach typically fare better with the Black community and brands. These churches are likely to have active ministries that branch into several areas of socio-economic support for their members and the surrounding community. Examples of this could be a ministry or nonprofit arm of the church that provides financial literacy for debt elimination, saving, and investing. Another is healthcare education based on partnerships with local healthcare providers. It's common to see various medical screenings happening onsite at the church, cancer or HIV survivor support groups, and forums for wellness and healthy eating. Other examples are youth and senior education classes for reading and computer literacy, credit counseling, and pathways to homeownership. Any and all of these ministries under the guidance of the church make a big impact and bring about relief and real change in the community.

Many Black Christians believe that Jesus Christ was a social justice advocate. However, teaching and practicing social justice in the church can be a slippery slope:

> "While the term social justice has become a convoluted one today, it is clearly defined throughout many passages of Scripture. Though the Scriptures don't speak directly of social justice, they do speak of the justice of God. Jesus quoted the Prophet Isaiah (Is 61:1–3) when he talked about taking care of the poor, prisoners, the blind, and the oppressed (Luke 4:18–19). According to Luke, Jesus was claiming to be the long-awaited Messiah. He was anointed to bring justice to the poor, prisoners, blind, and oppressed. This is just one example of God's idea of justice."[2]

Over the last few years, the Evangelical Movement has gone to great lengths to vilify any message from churches that connects with the social justice movement.[3] Evangelicals tend to be silent about mass incarceration and voters' rights, yet speak loudly against pre-marital sex, cohabitation without marriage, having children outside of marriage, and same-sex relationships. These practices have left youth, in particular, feeling judged, misplaced, and abandoned.

Conversely, the Black Church has endured the Evangelicals' interpretation and teachings of the Bible. There has been an ebb and flow, as well as a peculiar duality in the Black Church regarding the relationship between faith and social justice. On the one hand, religion, faith, and the Black Church have long been the source of foundation and strength in the Black community. Africans had to relatively quickly build solidarity with one another during the middle passage, despite them being from different nations, speaking different languages, and accustomed to different ways of life. Besides their Black skin color, newly transported slaves to American soil had little in common. Christianity, a new and, in some cases, strange religion, was the foundation of their coming together. During slavery and the life after, the Black Church has been a beacon of enduring hope. Having a deeply rooted sentiment for the poor and afflicted, the Black Church extends its reach to anyone who is marginalized and ostracized, including other minorities and migrants to America.

The Black Church provides counseling for families and individuals; resources for job training and jobs; medical and legal services; offender rehabilitation; food and school supply drives; support for single mothers, seniors, and more.

It has been the impetus for challenging mass incarceration and it often acts as a political nucleus to promote the importance of voting and voting rights. Black congregants profoundly benefit from all of the many ways the Black Church supports their everyday lives. The Black Church has stepped in to supplement and, in some cases, altogether replace the social, political, and economic needs of Black Americans with solutions that America has simply neglected for centuries. No wonder: "Most Black Christians say opposing racism is essential to being a Christian."[4]

Nevertheless, it's important to understand that there are some Black churches in alignment with the Evangelical Movement's practices.

Reverend Doctor Otis Moss, III, senior pastor at Trinity United Church of Christ in Chicago, explained the differences and similarities between Black and white churches during an interview for this book:

> "Black churches have their perspective, doctrines, practices, and rituals. The Black Church tradition is the centrality of Jesus. Yet, there are churches with Black people, but they don't necessarily follow the Black Church tradition, where the belief is that God has called us to liberate ourselves and to liberate all people."

The absence of these beliefs and customs also results in one of the most significant pain points that all churches face: membership retention.

According to a Barna Research study, church attendance across the country and for every generation of church members has demonstrated a steady decline in the past two decades. During this time, the "devout Christian" population has nearly dropped by half since 2000.[5] The Black Church has not eluded this downward trend, yet statistically, it is more likely to hold on to more congregants than churches frequented by the general population.

Millennials and Gen Zers undoubtedly influence these social changes. Their pursuit of justice and equality, which sometimes conflicts with the echoed rhetoric of the Evangelical's message of faith, is the primary reason for leaving the church. Dr. Moss shares information from Barna Research's church study and provides additional context about the Black youth mindset and their relationship with the church:

> "Rev. Brianna Parker (lead researcher for the Barna Research *State of the Black Church* Study[6]) has been doing work with Millennials and Gen Zers. She found that Black Generation Zers and Millennials have a higher view of Jesus than their parents. They have a higher view of what the faith tradition is supposed to do. . . . they have witnessed how the Black Church is borrowing from White evangelicalism tradition that creates the greatest kind of consternation with this generation."

How Americans Relate to Christianity is Changing: 2000–2020

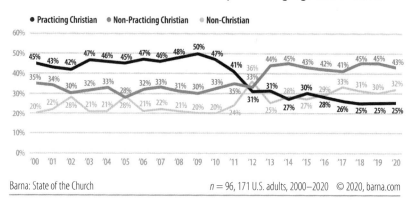

● Practicing Christian   ● Non-Practicing Christian   ● Non-Christian

Barna: State of the Church   *n* = 96, 171 U.S. adults, 2000–2020   © 2020, barna.com

Not ignoring this shift, some brands like P&G, Ben & Jerry's, and AARP have long understood the value of connecting with Black consumers. Their empathy-led strategies, targeted marketing, and communications efforts have bolstered successful advocacy, social justice, and cause-related initiatives.

For example, AARP wanted to connect with Black Church leaders to offer support and build a relationship with the Black community and increase its Black membership. While meeting with AARP executives in their Washington, D.C., corporate office for another project, I remember reading a wall plaque declaring AARP apolitical and its purpose as a social mission company.

That was a promising sign that an introduction to my church, Trinity United Church of Christ (under the leadership of Rev. Moss, mentioned earlier), would prove to be a win-win for both. The regional AARP division sponsored Trinity's literacy classes for Black men and the Jazzapolooza concerts for a few years. Dr. Moss invited an AARP outreach director to share the membership benefits with the congregation during Trinity's three Sunday services. Due to that invitation, congregants joined at a rate that more than tripled AARP's membership goal. This introduction was a successful demonstration that the winning approach for AARP regarding incorporating diverse markets is to partner with Black churches focusing on social justice.

✖

Trinity United Church of Christ–Chicago
On Solid Ground and Best in Class
Among (Black) Social-Justice Churches

A Brief History: Trinity's Foundation for Best in Class

Trinity United Church of Christ (Trinity) founded in 1961 in Chicago during the Civil Rights Movement, is a social-justice church that follows the doctrine of Jesus Christ, with the largest congregation in the United Church of Christ (UCC).

Part of the mission of the UCC embodies the principles of social justice. It mirrors the doctrines proclaimed by Jesus Christ, including fighting for the poor, the marginalized and underserved, and the practice of real inclusion. Historically in America, the UCC put a stake in the ground for social advocacy as far back as the 19th century. They were involved in the abolitionist and anti-slavery movements and played a pivotal role in the acquittal of the enslaved Africans accused of mutiny aboard the slave ship *Amistad*.

During Trinity's early years, overt perceptions about Black Christians were rampant, including the belief that Black Christians were inferior to white Christians.

These beliefs were welcomed and ubiquitous throughout the general church community across the country. And while it is less obvious today, Black believers are still perceived this way.

Under the short-term leadership of its third pastor, Reverend Ruben Sheares II (1971–1972), Trinity faced the challenge of needing to profess Christianity as a religion inclusive of Blacks. With only 259 members, Rev. Sheares met a divided Black Church community: those with aspirations for integration and assimilation and others who wanted a church home focused on Black pride and separation.

To set the stage, Rev. Sheares coined the creed "Unashamedly Black and Unapologetically Christian."[7] The Jesus-centric strategies were built around this slogan, and it resonated with the Black community. This was a seed planted, but at the time, not much change occurred.

From 1972 to 2008, Trinity was under the leadership of its fourth pastor, Reverend Doctor Jeremiah A. Wright, Jr., who passionately followed the doctrine of Jesus Christ under the auspice "to serve the least of these." He applied the "unashamedly Black and unapologetically Christian" motto as a guiding principle for the church and its members and encouraged parishioners to learn about religious, African, and American histories, as well as the significance of the Bible. Under his leadership, the congregation grew from 259 members to 6,500 **(including then-Democratic Presidential Nominee Barack Obama and his family*)**, plus over 70 active ministries.

Dr. Wright braved the trails of social justice on a faith-based platform that others feared. For example, in 1978, he authorized $100 to be spent on a "Free South Africa" sign and planted it in the churchyard until Nelson Mandela was freed. He urged other churches to buy "Free South Africa" signs in solidarity, but no other leaders joined in, he remembers.[8]

The divisiveness among the Black Church was strikingly apparent, but for the U.S., and globally, the urgency of social justice was certain.

*During Barack Obama's Democratic Nominee Campaign, Rev. Wright was condemned by national media for his fiery preaching style. Obama, under political pressure, withdrew himself from Trinity. In an attempt to educate the preaching styles of many Black ministers, allies of Rev Wright's continue to support him and the Black Church's style of worship:

"White America doesn't understand the Black Church, where themes of personal salvation and racial justice are often fused in a cathartic and boisterous call for redemption. Our brothers and sisters of European persuasion are suddenly paying attention to how we preach, and they don't understand it. They think it's harsh. They think it's bombastic. They believe (Wright) is a hate preacher. But if they, in their misunderstanding, visited most of our churches, they would think that that was true for us."

—**Rev. Dr. Calvin McKinney**, senior pastor
Calvary Baptist Church, Garfield, New Jersey

You cannot understand the African American preaching tradition unless you understand the African American church and how worshipers in this tradition demand that their preachers connect with them in a deeply emotional way as an integral part of their spirituality. This is true of the prosperity gospel of Bishop T.D. Jakes or the social (justice) gospel of Rev. Dr. Jeremiah Wright.

"The deep well of suffering in slavery, in lynching, in economic deprivation and separate and unequal schools and all the other travails of the African American experience have produced the African American worship context.

This context demands that its preachers deal with the whole of human life, it's terrible trials, and its unexpected miracles of triumph. And woe betides the preacher that does not address the full spectrum of truth from the pulpit in an African American church and does so passionately and articulately. "White America, this may not be the worship context you prefer and find most spiritually uplifting. This too should be respected. . . ."

—Susan Brooks Thistlethwaite, former president,
Chicago Theological Seminary (1998-2008), and
senior fellow at the Center for American Progress

In September 2016, Dr. Wright suffered a stroke that paralyzed the left side of his body. He is mobile by wheelchair and speaks softly, often only above a whisper. Despite the effect on his voice, Dr. Wright's legacy is loud and commands attention. He occasionally lectures, prepares sermons, and continues to be recognized for his work in the community and the nation, earning many outstanding-achievement awards.

Trinity Today: Effective Messaging, Outreach, and Growing Membership Contribute Mightily to Community Development

Since 2008, Trinity has been under the leadership of Reverend Dr. Otis Moss III. The alumni of Morehouse (political science), Yale (Master of Divinity), and Chicago Theological Seminary (Doctor of Ministry) forged ahead with the Jesus-centric social justice strategies and African associations.

Notably, Rev. Moss was comparably one of the youngest leaders (38 years old) of a large mega-church when he succeeded Dr. Wright. He understood the significance of pivoting to digital outreach to engage Black churchgoers long before COVID-19 restrictions forced people into it. He uses his dexterous communications expertise to provide Trinity's digital team with direction for well-crafted, cinematically relevant, and accessible digital content.

Today, Trinity connects with predominantly Black churchgoers using live and recorded video sermons and classes on multiple platforms. Members and visitors can access podcasts, relevant pop culture content, political forums, charitable giving opportunities and exclusive conversations with high-profile community leaders and celebrities like Denzel Washington. This progressive accessibility led to Trinity experiencing astronomical growth in the years before and throughout the COVID-19 pandemic. At this writing, Trinity embraces over 25,000 members worldwide.

Dr. Moss' legacy includes the community development project, Imani Village. Imani Village is a social enterprise developed for the empowerment of underserved and historically disenfranchised residents of the Pullman Community and the surrounding neighborhoods of Chicago, Illinois. The Village represents a unique collaboration between the faith community, local government, and business interests, to provide a model for urban planning and development that delivers a sustainable green infrastructure, jobs and job training, healthy urban lifestyle alternatives, and an optimized educational environment.

Imani Village will be home to an Education Innovation & Youth Development Center—educating Black children at the highest level, with a curriculum delivered from a culturally relevant perspective. It will also feature sustainable housing with intentional Green design elements to lower electricity and heating costs, and protect the environment.

The Village plan also includes an organic community garden—providing a source of healthy food alternatives for one of the food deserts of the Southside—along with an urban farming and agricultural center that will educate and employ community residents.

Other offerings include a NCAA-certified sports complex for tennis, track, football, soccer, basketball, and lacrosse; and a retail center providing community employment and consumer goods for the entire village. The plan also includes a community health center that will deliver much-needed services to an under-served area of the city.

Dr. Moss tells me that the project will likely be completed long after his retirement, yet the principles for Imani Village follow the basic principles of Trinity in that:

1. Contractors must be from the community to empower the community and make sure those dollars circulate in the community.

2. The architectural design has to be green.

3. Those working on the development have to include returning citizens from the mass incarceration system.

Dr. Moss' vision is to continue to use video content and storytelling to educate its members about America's history and unvarnished truth. In 2020, during the pandemic, he co-wrote and produced the film *Otis' Dream*, which tells the story of his grandfather, Otis Moss, Senior, a southern farmer with five children whose dream was to vote. According to Dr. Moss, the film has been viewed over a million times. Hosea Sanders, an anchor for ABC News Chicago, writes about some of the film's awards on the station's website:

> "*Otis' Dream* and its message has been lauded by luminaries, including Oprah Winfrey, and now this local production is racking up awards on the festival circuit, including one in the UK, I Will Tell International Films, and a Chicago Independent Film award . . ."

Notes

1. "African American Worship: It's Heritage, Character and Quality," ministymagazine.org, Sept. 2002

2. "The Role of the Black Church and Social Justice," UKessays.com, 5/18/2020

3. *Ibid.*

4. "The Black Church is having a moment," John Black and Beesheer Mohammed, senior researcher, The Pew Center, CNN.com, 2/16/2021

5. Barna.com, 2020

6. *Ibid.*

7. The History of Trinity United Church of Christ, trinitychicago.org/the-history-of-trinity/

8. "Chicago activists who never gave up on a Free South Africa," Ufrieda Ho, newframe.com, 4/27/21

18

Modern Black Grassroots Events Foster Acceptance

Rarely are Black brands created to exclude anyone. They're created for the precise purpose of inclusion. These brands are made because entire American consumer groups are absent from the table, misrepresented, if at all, and ultimately factored out.

Black Americans' go-to has always been grassroots. Promoting ideas within the community using grassroots methods has been a cornerstone of the Black American experience since slavery.

Examples of modern grassroots events that are redefining cultural norms can be found in organizations and brands that have sprung up in the past ten years, usually with some indication in their name that it is "for" Black consumers. Clients often ask for recommendations for Black events. In response, I would rattle off a few names, some would be familiar, but many were not, and at that point, the clients would respond, *"I didn't know."* I've listed a few of the popular events and a few that have great cultural connections with the Black community yet are under business leaders' radar.

AfroTech

AfroTech, founded in 2014, solved the unmet needs of Black tech innovators, entrepreneurs and subject-matter enthusiasts when they launched a news site. It was created by Morgan DeBaun, founder and CEO of Blavity, Inc. Her company is home to the largest network of platforms and lifestyle brands serving the multifaceted lives of Black Millennials.

AfroTech has quickly grown into a behemoth, becoming the largest Black tech conference of the year. It was developed for the Black community, but does not exclude anyone. According to DeBaun: "We design AFROTECH for the Black community and those who support Black advancement in professional spaces . . . that's my target demo and that's what we design for. And from the music, to the color scheme to the food at the food trucks, to the speakers, we are unapologetically Black all the way through."[1]

Imagine an abundance of highly educated, highly influential, innovative Black founders, CEOs, investors and influencers in one space. And while the event is about business and technology, transcending race. Black is at the center of the experience. Black-centric experiences in and of themselves are varied and unique because Black culture is a kaleidoscope of experiences and exposure. This conference provides a full week of presentations, panel discussions, music, networking and recruiting opportunities.

One might find conference goers in fine-cut European suits, stately African garb or casual skinny jeans and tees. Some of the most unassuming individuals could be multi-millionaire tech founders or young coders with groundbreaking ideas, both looking for a place to belong. Here, there is no question of representation; carving out space for Black thinkers and doers in this category is what AfroTech has achieved.

DeBaun further explains that there is no need for explaining who Black techs are or the Black experience, but rather: *"Should I be using Kubernetes in my code?"* Or, *"How do I become a director at my company"* Or, *"How do I get on the board at this company? Or, "How do I ace that interview?"*[2]

AFROPUNK

James Spooner filmed a documentary, *Afro-Punk,* in 2003 featuring the lives of four African Americans dedicated to the punk rock lifestyle. As a music genre and subculture, atypical to that of most Black Americans, the film examined the exile and loneliness felt by these Black punk rockers, while also exploring the unfamiliar territory of interracial dating and what Black power looked like for them. Spooner founded AfroPunk, alongside co-founder Matthew Morgan in 2005. The local Brooklyn-based festival featured music, arts, film, and fashion for Black Americans who needed an event to experience and express their lifestyle with like-minded individuals.

Almost a decade later, AFROPUNK grew in popularity around 2014 when Millennial influencers began to attend and share the event with their followers. During a time when many social media platforms were popping up, showcasing Black in a positive light, AFROPUNK amplified "Black cool" by showing Black festival goers in full Black pride: Big epic afros, long locs, majestic beards, artful tattoos, regal piercings, stylish fashion and authentic music commanded attention.

Their grassroots influence led to the festival taking the event international in 2015, with additional festivals in Johannesburg, Paris, Atlanta, and London. It has become a global cultural shape-shifting celebration attended by thousands of multicultural youth where you see both everyday individuals and celebrities bringing their personal yet Black-influenced experiences to the festival via unapologetic styles of self-expression. These are the artists, influencers, and creatives who were once seen as outsiders but now directly affect pop culture worldwide.

AFROPUNK expanded its platform not only to represent music, but Black culture, fashion, activism, and wellness. *Solution Sessions,* AFROPUNK's signature community activism platform, uses the spirit and power of community to tackle important conversations about how culture, activism, and politics impact folks of color and solutions that achieve positive results.[3]

Essence Festival

The Essence Festival of Culture (Essence Fest), is an annual music festival that started in 1995 as a one-time event to celebrate the 25th anniversary of *Essence*, a magazine aimed primarily at Black American women. It became the largest Black American culture and music event in the United States. The popular event has been held every Fourth of July weekend in New Orleans, since its inception, except for 2006 when it was held in Houston following Hurricane Katrina (August 2005).

Essence Fest is known for its nonstop live music featuring some of the best in R&B, soul, funk, gospel, and Hip-Hop. Some of the past big-name artists that have headlined the fest include Beyoncé, Mary J. Blige, Patti LaBelle, Janet Jackson, Yolanda Adams, Kevin Hart, and Nicki Minaj, among others.

Often referred to as "a party with a purpose," seminars and workshops are also a big attraction to the fest. Attendees can bolster their knowledge and confidence via the Essence Expo Experience, which includes seminars, live tutorials, free consultations, and workshops on a wide range of topics, including beauty and style, power, entrepreneurship and finance, as well as health, wellness, spirituality, and much more.[4] Essence has welcomed celebrity speakers and panelists to enhance the motivational experience. The list of prominent speakers includes Oprah, former First Lady Michelle Obama, Gayle King, Iyanla Vanzant, Tamron Hall, Dr. Michael Eric Dyson, and many others.

TSP: Traffic Sales and Profit

Lamar and Ronnie Tyler are beasts! This husband and wife team first gained visibility from the success of their nationwide Black community parenting platform, Blackandmarriedwithkids.com. They owned the business for years and sold it in 2022 to two of their clients.

Prior to selling the business, they parlayed dollars from that business to create the highly acclaimed and wildly successful media business, TSP—Traffic Sales and Profit. Through in-person and online conferences, training, and mentorship, TSP targets Black entrepreneurs and future business owners. The Tylers are driven to help Black entrepreneurs succeed, and their reputation of being smart and buttoned up precedes them.

They invite the best and brightest as keynotes to train and participate in video interviews and podcasts, from young successful bootstrap entrepreneurs to Harvard MBAs. At the 2022 conference they welcomed

Magic Johnson! No doubt that in the future, more celebrities like Magic will be onboard.

They stay connected with their audience of thousands by using a down-to-earth, matter-of-fact, no-nonsense, yet an honest approach to successful business strategies. They offer memberships at various levels and position pricing via added value messaging.

I had the opportunity to present Black insights at their 2020 conference when COVID restrictions were lifting. Being attentive to COVID safety practices, they limited attendees to 300 people (vs. 750). There were also 800+ people online—all happily paid a few hundred dollars for the registration.

They are masters at pushing out content. They are everywhere on social media: YouTube, Instagram, Twitter, Linked-In, Facebook, Apple Podcasts, and short videos on TikTok. The digital campaigns of emails and video interviews of successful Black business owners welcome, inspire and motivate their audience. They understand the struggles of the Black entrepreneur but don't linger in that space. Lamar is the face of TSP and delivers a "we got you, you can do this" upbeat message onstage and on video.

The Tylers have been at this for a few years, and what is also particularly interesting is how they have taken the FUBU concept mentioned earlier (For Us By Us), to a new level. As of this writing, they have not accepted any sponsorships. The Tylers are not anti-sponsorship but believe it's essential first to stay true to their mission, as explained by Lamar: "We haven't found a partner that values what we bring, and yet have been able to fully monetize the events without sponsorship dollars."

The Megafest Beer Festival, Washington, D.C.

Being Howard University alums was one commonality that made it easy for Brandon Miller and Elliott Johnson to get on well after meeting for the first time in 2018. Sometime after, friendly conversations turned to business when Miller initiated the idea of working together. Johnson is the CEO and co-founder of Soul Mega Brewing. Miller is the event director with The Usual Suspectz, a national marketing company providing entertainment-related services and events targeting Black Millennials. Their experience aligns perfectly with event opportunities, so they collaboratively built the idea of the MegaFest Beer Festival.

Given that Black-owned breweries are challenged for exposure, Miller and Johnson were fully entrenched with the idea to showcase multiple Black-owned breweries exclusively. Additionally, the creators wanted to inject positive realism into the mix through the eyes of Black culture. Whites were welcomed, and some attended, but the event had to scream "for us, by us." MegaFest premiered in August 2022. Six Black-owned breweries participated. It was very successful. They anticipated and welcomed between 500-600 visitors and received a big shout-out from *The Washington Post.*[5]

During a phone interview, Brandon Miller shared this with me: "We wanted to do something different from mainstream beer events. It was important to not only feature Black breweries, but the event also needed to look different, sound different, and feel different. We created a space that provided a "Black block party" feel, with down-home food, and "house music" because it is consistently fun and upbeat. It was well-attended and the first of its kind in D.C., with more to come in the future."

The Black Women's Expo

In 1993, the show then titled "An Expo for Today's Black Woman," was primarily focused on providing an annual event that allowed small businesses and major corporations to showcase their products and services before African American consumers in the Chicagoland area. Today, the Black Women's Expo, also known as BWe NEXT, has evolved into the largest lifestyle exposition for Black women in the country. Merry Green, BWe CEO, holds the event in three markets—Chicago, Detroit, and Atlanta. Green ensures that BWe provides a platform where the societal issues faced cannot only be amplified but tackled!

In each market, the weekend exposition on-site is comprised of small and large activations that address the needs of Black women and their families—via topical seminars and general sessions presented by a five-star roster of subject matter experts, themed resource pavilions (health & wellness, food & nutrition, finance and generational wealth, business ownership, and much more), a small business exhibitor's marketplace, and corporate exhibitions on the main floor.

BWe has been the nation's longest-running, most-respected, intergenerational exposition targeting Black Women and their families—where hundreds of women gather to share ideas, search for solutions, grow their businesses, and where corporate brands can speak directly to this consumer.[6]

Why Black Community Matters in Marketing

Black Americans do have and desire a strong sense of belonging and community. Any messaging that attempts to exclude a group of us or doesn't portray participants as happy, supporting one another, and progressing, will be met with criticism.

Mainstream media has often perpetuated the belief that Black people are a disjointed culture of people; that we don't support one another and that we tear each other down. This sentiment has even reverberated throughout our communities by Black people themselves. But it's just not true. Black consumers support Black businesses and important causes.

Black consumers engage in Black and mainstream news. Black consumers celebrate the success of other Black friends, family, and public figures. Black consumers desire a tribe, keep their community close, and celebrate togetherness.

●

THE OPPORTUNITY

For marketers who want to make a sincere and impactful campaign that targets these connected people, finding ways to contribute to the community can be a sound strategy to start. Elements of culture born of Black folks often begins in small spaces. These spaces are our communities. And in a world where safety and acceptance can hardly ever be certain, our communities are the places where we can be our true selves.

●

Notes

1. "The Largest Black Tech Conference Is Back: Morgan DeBaun Shares What This Year's AFROTECH Will Bring," Janice Gassam Asare, *Forbes*, 11/10/2022

2. *Ibid.*

3. Afropunk.com/solution sessions

4. Neworleans.com/things to do

5. "A New Festival Celebrates Black-owned Beers with a 'Block-party Vibe,'" Fritz Hahn, *The Washington Post*, 8/25/2022

6. Bwenext.com

19

Black Media

Valuable, Relevant, and Here to Stay

When Johnson Publishing sold its iconic brand, *Ebony Magazine,* to a private firm in 2016, a sense of loss reverberated across the Black community, young and old. *Ebony,* founded by the late John H. Johnson, chronicled Black life for over seventy years; a mainstay through the eras that showed Black people as they saw themselves—beautiful, successful, progressive, altruistic, educated, enterprising, family-oriented, stylish, fashionable, and overcomers. Johnson, thought of by many as a brilliant and stringent leader, would say that he "pulled himself up by his bootstraps" to launch that first issue of *Ebony* on November 1, 1945. The magazine told the generation's stories then and stayed relevant as the years and decades went by. Newer generations inherited a reverence for the beloved publication because a copy lay topmost on every stack of magazines on grandma's coffee table, at the beauty salon or barber shop, or in their doctor's waiting room. Inside, the bold type, polished graphics, natural beauties, latest fashion and buzz on trends, and celebrity news were something to be marveled at; and this all conveyed an important message that Black is beautiful, powerful, desirable, and worthy of recognition.

Over one hundred years ago, long before *Ebony Magazine,* it was apparent that Black media held significant value back in the 19th century. When a group of free Black men in New York City founded *Freedom's Journal,* the publication of its first issue in March 1827 made it the first newspaper owned by, led by, and written for Black Americans in the United States.[1] It was the beginning of expressing and publishing the Black narrative. The result: a well-established, informational, empowering, and celebratory publication centering the Black community.

Today, many decision-makers take Black media for granted. They misunderstand Black identity, Black language, and the importance of broadcasting Black progress.

Structurally, Black media is no different than mainstream media. There are print, TV, radio, podcasts, digital publications and social-media platforms, as well as web, mobile apps, gaming and eCommerce. Print publications, especially small local ones, suffer the most from declining revenue as advertisers shift media budgets to the digital space—again, much like mainstream. But the difference is that statistically, small Black publishers and broadcasters have always gotten the shortest end of the stick. If any credence and market spend is to be allocated in the Black media category, the thought-process is that there can only be one giant that represents them all. There are multiple television networks Black people tune into, and in which agencies could spend ad dollars.

Rapidly changing technology and lifestyles, the information-saturated digital era, and declining capital have forced most Black media companies to pivot to online platforms where frequency and market reach isn't a limitation. But staying in the black continues to be a struggle.

At the same time, we see that new Black publications—and Black media startups in general—launch every year, which shows the need and demand for Black voices and perspectives. Black consumers are looking for representation in the typical areas of entertainment, sports, current events, pop culture, politics, health, wellness, beauty, and finance. But also in other sectors that aren't thought to be of interest to Black consumers, like entrepreneurship, science, medicine, technology, gaming, design, architecture, travel, culinary arts, and horticulture. In Chicago, Yvette Moyo and her company, Real Men Charities, launched *South Side*

Drive in 2020. This magazine aims to catalyze economic development in predominantly Black communities on Chicago's south side. In so doing, Moyo is intentional about countering the negative stories about Chicago, like the shootings and car-jackings that dominate the news. A newer publication, *Chicago News Weekly,* was launched in the fall of 2022; it covers the most relevant news and events affecting Chicago's progressive Black Community. The platform includes traditional articles, as well as streaming content, videos, and original programming.

Why Black Media Matters

We in the industry know that media broadcasting and publications can't stay afloat through subscribership only. Strategic advertising and promotional partnerships support any company's launch and expansion. Black media matters now more than ever because Black consumers want stories, events, and cultural connections from the Black perspective. More than anything, they know that Black media won't leave them out. The challenge is maintaining a competitive market share and reach. In doing so, Black media must keep up with advancing technologies and sustain a well-supported staff that can keep pace with the demand for relevant contemporary content.

Despite these challenges, on-point Black media continues to be embraced as valuable, relevant, and here to stay. Here's what the marketing and media industries miss when they pass over Black media opportunities in television, radio, print, and digital:

- Black media's most important asset is the ability to recount our stories and our truths in our authentic voices. Authentic stories heralded by Black storytellers center the Black experience from an authentic perspective. They validate us. They say what we're thinking, they affirm what we believe. They also challenge new perspectives and call our attention to urgent and relevant happenings.
- While Black storytellers and their platforms want to outshine the negativity that often exists about them in mainstream media,

Black media isn't entirely about countering negative stereotypes. It's mostly about reveling in what it means to be "us"—the humor, the struggles, the affirmations, the progress, and the joys of being Black.

- In Black-owned and Black-led publications and productions, there isn't a need to ask, "well, what about me?" Black is at the center—and for Black Americans who are often marginalized by mainstream media, being at the center feels good.

Detavio Samuels, CEO of REVOLT.TV has been an enduring champion of Black media and has worked on casting a big picture for what it could become. REVOLT.TV provides space for Black culture's unfiltered conversations in an authoritative voice about music, including rap and R&B, as well as social-justice news, pop culture, and other issues of interest to its Black audience. One such production by the network is "Drink Champs," the "popular unpopular music podcast." According to *The New Yorker,* "despite its exorbitant length, Drink Champs' success flows partly from its A-list guests, who are drawn from Hip-Hop history: Grandmaster Caz, Lil Wayne, and Snoop Dogg." N.O.R.E., formerly Noreaga, an American Hip-Hop and Reggaeton recording artist, and Capone, a rapper from Queens, New York, are the hosts. N.O.R.E is often credited for getting interviews with certain celebrities and public figures that most hosts can't.

Listeners who may not be the target audience may feel squeamish about the language and tone of conversation during these interviews. Yet, the stories these artists share often include experiences, struggles, and victories, which are inspiring and relatable to people in the culture. Notably, many interviewees from Hip-Hop backgrounds have impressive business acumen. It's not uncommon to hear these celebrities discuss the importance of mentoring, networking, saving, and investing. They inspire their audience to do the same.

In several podcast interviews and live panel discussions, Samuels (an older Millennial) is passionate about helping the Black community.

The media and marketing industries understand the importance of controlling the Black narrative in the Black voice.

One of my favorite Samuels interviews is on the Geekset Podcast,[2] with host Rudy "Young Deuces" Strong. In it, Samuels shares his perspective on two quotes of historical origins and his interpretation of how these quotes underscore Black media's value in controlling the Black community's story:

> **Plato quote:** *Those who write stories rule society.*

> **Samuels' insight:** If you aren't offering the narrative, you can't run the world. Whoever owns the dominant record becomes the truth.

> **African Proverb:** *Until the lion learns to tell his history, the tale of the hunt will always glorify the hunter.*

> **Samuels' insight:** We live in a world where the hunter has always been glorified. So, Black media matters because you have to take the pen and put it in the hand of the lion and let the lion tell his own story. Media is simply an industry of ideas, and if you are not the one putting ideas into this world and into this earth, then you are merely a victim, left with whatever people say about you.

Additionally, Šesali Bowen, author of *Bad, Fat, Black Girl,* writes for film and television. One of her pieces for the paramount.com television network underscored a particular occasion when Black Twitter and BET joined forces to tell a great story about the BET Awards. Bowen also gives major props to BET for its history of validating Black people globally by telling Black truths:

> "From music and politics to art and lifestyle, the network has been aggregating the stories and history of people all over the Black diaspora over the course of its 40+-year history. BET has built the trust of Black folks as a hub for mainstream Black culture by doing its best to let Black people spit their own truth—fighting against a tide of erasure, vilification, tokenization, and caricaturization at other media outlets."[3]

Let Me Explain Black *Media Value* . . .

Let's delve into the specific ways in which Black media proves to be a valuable staple in the Black American experience.

Valued for Trust

During the early days of the onset of COVID-19 in the United States, Black Americans were dying at highly disproportionate rates when compared to any other racial group in the country. The collective Black media—print, radio, Black social media, and Black email marketers made a concerted effort to emphasize the gravity of the pandemic and its effects on the community's mothers, husbands, sons, daughters, elders, and children. In fact, concerning coverage of COVID-19, Black media wrote five times more than mainstream media on the disproportionate racial impact of the pandemic and nearly twice as much as mainstream media on the frontline and essential workers.[4]

Email and mobile marketers who target the Black audience are essential in the Black-media discussion, yet they exist under the radar. Support overall is slim, yet they amplify voices and stories not covered in mainstream media. During COVID-19, they too were instrumental in helping the Black community understand the severity of the pandemic and offered tips and information on how to spot symptoms, how to get tested, the importance of sheltering in place, and how to best protect yourself if you were deemed one of America's "essential workers." The Ujaama Network was unceasingly spreading the news about the importance of masking during the early days and months of the pandemic. The network's owner, Mike House, often shared quick-read copy, infographics, and illustrations about mask varieties, expert recommendations, and how to wear them correctly.

As the months progressed, Black media began to connect the dots between health and healthcare disparities in communities of color, to the broken healthcare system in America, and how it specifically painted a dismal picture for Black people during the outbreak. But it also high-lighted disparities that stretched back decades before COVID-19. These stories were first posted on Black and social media channels weeks before we saw some mention of it in mainstream media.

The COVID-19 pandemic, alongside the unprecedented George Floyd protests, was a *lightbulb moment* that sent many healthcare leaders my way. In light of this new information, their interest in the Black community led to my firm conducting Black patient research, Black insights keynote presentations, and workshops. These were insurance and pharmaceutical companies and hospitals eager to better understand the Black experience and their healthcare journey.

Trust is also imbued in Black media because Black storytellers report the facts from a basis and lens of humanity. Black consumers can trust that Black media has Black lives, health and wellness, and their best overall interest in mind.

So there's no confusion . . .

Black media uses the word "Black" in coverage, explicitly utilizing Black to indicate a person, community, or group, as well as business, sports, healthcare, or any other topic when reporting the news. It is consistently the most frequently used word in the top 100 words and is uniquely prominent in news coverage compared to the top words used by mainstream media. Further, Black media accurately call people killed by police brutality victims, sons and daughters,rather than calling a Black adolescent boy "a Black man," or communities of displaced American residents "refugees."[5] It accurately portrays Black people for the first time without retracting or rephrasing its original coverage, as we see so often in mainstream media. When a white or non-Black assailant commits a crime against a group of individuals in the United States, Black media, by definition, calls that individual a terrorist. When a Black individual is involved in an incident that is being investigated, they often use less threatening or incriminating images of that individual. When Black

Americans are victims of a crime or injustice, Black media tells that story as such. You must imagine that feels good, too.

Does mainstream news benefit or thrive off the negative experiences of Black Americans?

In an article by Liz Nass: *The Fight for African American Representation in Media,* Daniela Bondekwe, a neuroscience student and campus writer for *Black Media Entertainment,* discusses how mainstream news depicts Black Americans. She writes:

> "The problem with mainstream news is generalizations. Journalism has had moments where it has depicted African Americans negatively and often has thrived off African Americans' negative experience . . . to reiterate some stereotypes."

Valued for Relevant Information

Why Black Media Matters is a project of the Black Media Initiative conducted by the Center for Community Media at the City University of New York's Craig Newmark Graduate School of Journalism.

The report "Why Black Media Matters Now" analyzed the coverage of nearly 100 Black-owned news outlets over 15 months between March 2020 and May 2021. Below, I highlight a few of the rich findings from that report related to valued news and information provided by Black media:

- Black media publishes, by a factor of as high as six times, more coverage than mainstream media on issues of importance to Black communities, including racism, health disparities, and voting access.
- Nearly one in every four (23%) articles in Black media mentioned racism or related issues, compared to less than one in ten (8%) in mainstream media.
- Black media covered health issues of particular relevance to Black

communities at higher levels than mainstream media, including maternal health, hypertension, diabetes, HIV/AIDS, and sickle cell disease.

- The issue of voting access was included in 12 percent of all political stories in Black media, which is more than twice the percentage for mainstream media (5 percent).

- Black media provides historical context to present-day challenges. This is done by explicitly including historical events in related breaking news, and by linking related news events, such as police killings of Black people, to breaking stories.

- Black media cover Africa and other countries of the African diaspora more than mainstream media. In fact, during the 2021 focus groups that we conducted with Black network news watchers, we learned that U.S. and international news about the African diaspora is important to these viewers.

Valued for Advocating Justice & Breaking News

Black media have continued to advocate for Black-related justice in police and law enforcement, the justice system, and politics/voting to counteract non-reported, underreported, or inaccurate information concerning Black communities on these subjects. Compare the coverage between Black and mainstream news coverage (especially in the beginning periods) of Hurricane Katrina, Trayvon Martin, Freddie Gray, Ahmaud Arbery, Breonna Taylor, and the effects of COVID-19 in the Black community. In addition to a lack of coverage, mainstream news also misses the mark concerning big-picture issues and how these individual incidents contribute to a larger problem for Black Americans. Even after the death of George Floyd, mainstream media did not connect these issues to voting and justice as the Black press did.[6]

The emphasis on Black media reporting at an earlier rate in the news cycle than mainstream outlets is essential. Often, these stories are of an urgent nature, and disseminating the information to the masses is critical. They would qualify as breaking . . . for some but not for others. By the time mainstream news picks up the story—only after Black and minority-focused platforms have garnered the attention of thousands, if not millions—the message is clear: Black stories, even the dangerous or urgent ones, aren't important for mainstream coverage and consumption unless there is a clear interest in numbers, or an obvious grab for clicks, likes—and a payoff on ad spends.

Value for Emotional and Cultural Commitment

The emotional and cultural commitment that Black media provides Black consumers gives them a sense of belonging, being desired and also being understood. These qualities are nuanced and therefore when the commitment is present, it gives, again, that authentic factor that has such a strong intrinsic value. While African Americans are indeed American, and speak English, a commitment to Black culture and the emotional journey of Black people makes a big impact on not just attracting these audiences to a particular platform but giving them a grounded reason for coming back over and over again, making them loyal readers, listeners, and viewers.

The emotional and cultural value in Black media is highly misjudged and underestimated. As discussed in earlier chapters, *"They speak English, don't they?"* is the business leaders' blind spot—their rationale for not investing in Black media, and a barrier to connecting with a loyal audience.

Alfred Edmond, Jr., SVP and executive editor-at-large of *Black Enterprise,* spoke with me about the emotional attachment Black media has with the Black community and the work *Black Enterprise* has been doing to foster trust with their brand:

> "We understand and appreciate Black people's stake in Black media and have been making the trust and value case for years by being relevant and relatable. We've pivoted from the physical magazine and focused more on customized events that provide helpful information

and reflect the best of who the Black business community is. Black Enterprise is like the Good Housekeeping Seal of Approval. It validates and adds credibility to Black culture."

Another example of cultural attachment involves the Black traveler. Black business-and-leisure travel domestically and internationally continues to rise yearly. Black travelers in the U.S. spend upwards of $129 billion annually on domestic and international travel. Even though Black faces, individuals, families, and business-oriented representation aren't evident in advertising, the numbers tell a strong story for Black travel and their stake in the game. It smashes negative stereotypes that Black travelers aren't pioneers, swimmers, pilots, accommodation owners . . . the list goes on and on.[7] When Blacks travel, they take their culture with them. So, when the travel industry didn't speak to the image and experience of Black travelers, Zim Ugochukwu stepped up and founded Travel Noire in 2013. She launched the social-media platform and website as a community for young Black Millennial travelers to share their travel stories. It morphed into a platform with international tour services, interactive city guides and tools for travel.[8]

In 2017, Blavity purchased Travel Noire, and since the launch of Travel Noire, several platforms, publications and similar startups have been produced with the Black traveler in mind.

The Ongoing Struggle: Efficiency vs. Effectiveness

Black media is in a precarious position of balancing efficiency with the need for maximum effectiveness. For decades Black media have encountered roller-coaster conditions when attempting to acquire and maintain advertising and promotional partnerships. Only 2 percent of total media spend is allocated to Black media. Some of the critical reasons for ad spend rejection include:

- The belief that reaching Black consumers through mainstream media is sufficient

- The perception that Black media lacks adequate reach
- Lack of familiarity with Black media

One of the biggest hurdles to overcome, especially for local Black media, is satisfying advertisers' standards for efficiency. An efficient media outlet promises to reach more people while being mindful of the costs. However, low-volume ad spending means higher costs per ad or per click. It's a tough spot to be in. Nevertheless, the effectiveness of Black media hasn't wavered.

In addition to being a trusted source of news and information, the most compelling evidence of Black media's effectiveness is its grassroots benefits, a unique attribute that sets it apart from mainstream media.

First, it's important to make a side note that Black Americans indeed use mainstream media, while embracing Black media. The duality, in simple terms, is that Black media brings cultural, emotional and practical relevance to Black audiences and mainstream media provides a generally prevalent and ubiquitous nature on pressing issues, yet it tends to operate on the periphery of Black communities. The grassroots factor, however, brings a new level of value to the media topic. The grassroots influence that defines, depicts, and speaks to the Black population at large can penetrate that periphery and dismantle it.

The grassroots factor reaches and authentically engages the Black community with relevant content and a compelling take on culture and community—AND its undeniable influence and powerful fanfare often make it to the desks and screens of mainstream America. Grassroots magnifies everything, making its subject a hot topic, the most influential trend, or the most pressing news piece of the moment. It garners the attention of the masses and compels everyone to get on board. Grassroots sets trends and catalyzes movements. Think Black Lives Matter or even the candidacy of then-Senator Barack Obama—grassroots movements are partly or primarily responsible for launching that movement and his presidency, respectively. This is the unique effect that's hard to duplicate or fabricate. And Black media has it in the bag.

I like to say, "back in the day," Black agencies understood the power of Black media without a second thought. Investing in Black media was a no-brainer when they had the authority to purchase advertising for their clients in Black media categories. Media buying under the direction of Black agencies has shifted to general media buying agencies and has negatively impacted both—Black media agencies and Black media. For example, between 2000 and 2015, Black print newspaper ad revenues fell from approximately $60 billion to $20 billion.[9] Black-owned agencies' income suffered a loss of 17.5 percent in commission.

In an article he wrote for *Adweek*, "Black-Owned Ad Agencies Need Their Buying Power Back," Don Moore, chief executive officer and president of Hybrid Theory, North America, shares insights from his conversation with media consultant Deborah Gray Young, including her comments about Black agencies purchasing Black media:

> "Whether it was retail, QSR (Quick Service Restaurants), or automotive, Black-owned agencies in their heyday knew the brands, as well as they knew their consumers—with creative and media planning and buying under one roof, they were able to put deals together that provided maximum value and unquestioned authenticity for the Black community at large. This kind of synergy played a crucial role in keeping Black-owned media."

The traditional media buying process back then, even a decade ago, was different from the current process. According to adjust.com, this process involved a considerable amount of manual work, typically with several requests for proposals (RFPs), account manager negotiations, and manual insertions of the orders (IOs), which made it slow and inefficient. Today, the technology of programmatic advertising media buying is automated, using data insights and algorithms to deliver ads to the right user at the right time and price. This process has replaced the traditional manual process, and yes, it's more efficient. But at what cost? Automation has taken center stage in identifying and determining which media brands meet its standards. Marketers who ignore the compelling benefits of Black media and the value that Black agencies bring to the media buying table are probably replacing effectiveness with efficiency.

Efficiency vs. Effectiveness

Malcolm Devoy, EMEA chief strategy officer at London-based Ph.D. and co-author of *Overthrow II: 10 Strategies from the New Wave of Challengers,* explains it well:

> "Brands can be efficient by being effective. But the relationship doesn't hold the other way around—brands don't tend to become effective by being efficient. The sooner we correct our linguistic mistake that efficiency equals effectiveness, the sooner clients will start to get the effective media strategies they need."

Brands Are Independently Stepping Up

Following George Floyd's murder and the ensuing protests, several brand alliances have pledged to spend at least two percent of their total brands' ad-spend budget with Black media.

Publicis Media announced the launch of the Once & For All Coalition, a two-year initiative with a three-fold mission: to tackle the removal of barriers to financially support minority-owned media, to invest in a range of content, and to create guidelines of best practices to invest in them directly. The coalition consists of 21 of Publicis' clients (open to all of Publicis' clients, which include Best Buy, GSK, Yum Brands, J.M. Smucker Co., and others) as well as 23 primarily Black and Hispanic traditional and emerging media companies (including Black Enterprise, iHeart Media, and Univision).

The challenge has been the industry's consensus around what defines minority-owned media. Brands also want to ensure they're not only spending on minority-owned [companies] but have a reasonable and equitable spend in minority-targeted . . . and minority-operated media.

The Association for National Advertisers (ANA)-backed Alliance for Inclusive and Multicultural Marketing (AIMM) is also involved. In fact, following George Floyd's murder, they pledged to "do everything in our individual and collective power to end systemic racism and achieve equality and justice" in the marketing and advertising industries. This pledge was signed by their board of directors and senior-level corporate members from brands, media companies, research firms, industry groups, and agencies. An ad was created from this "manifesto" and ran in *The New York Times*. Today, they are actively leading the DEI pledge via the ANA Growth Agenda—a growth strategy with four growth priorities and 12 focus areas.

GroupM aims to make its media buying and planning more responsible and purposeful. Earlier in 2022, the media agency unveiled its new 2-percent-plus pledge, which aims to get clients to spend at least 2 percent of their media dollars with Black-owned media brands, according to digday.com.

Another significant promise is from Marc Pritchard, P&G's chief brand officer. He publicly pledged to set P&G's weekly goal to reach 80 to 90 percent of multicultural consumers.[10]

It is uncertain how consistent these pledges will be in the long term. To scale and sustain their businesses, Black-owned-and-operated media need advertising and promotional partnerships that bring in the revenue necessary for fast, relevant, and effective content creation.

Blacklisted Words

Social media is especially culpable for blacklisting words that have cultural relevance to the Black community . . . like *Black*, for example!

In an interview for Lucinda Southern's article for digday.com titled "Time to put their money where their mouth is: Minority community publishers hurt worse by keyword blocking," Brand Advance CEO Christopher Kenna explains the problems associated with blacklisted words and minority segments, demographics, and why psychographics must be included in targeting: "Brands should get to choose where their ads appear, but blanket blocking is not a brand taking a stand; it's just lazy."

"Brands need to revisit their blocklists and consider if they are discriminative," said a U.K. news publisher. "Words such as 'Black,' 'LGBTQ' or 'Muslim' should never feature on a blocklist but often do, having been put there five years ago," the publisher said. "Brands concerned about words such as 'lesbian' for fear of being on a porn site should probably check their lists rather than demonize a section of society."

Bottom Line

From being last to have coverage, to being blacklisted, Black agencies understand and have sound motives for propelling Black culture forward. I compel non-Black agencies to incorporate Black media into their strategy, if Black consumer loyalty is important to their bottom line. But my bottom line here, is a call for Black agencies to take back the wheel, get back in the driver's seat and buy Black media.

Best Practice
PRIDE Magazine—Charlotte, North Carolina

In an era where single or regional market print magazines—especially Black ones—struggle, *PRIDE Magazine* has survived and thrived for 30 years.[11]

Dee Dixon is recognized in the Charlotte community for her distinctive flat-top natural hairstyle as well as her contributions to the Black community. Dee is the owner and CEO of Pride Communications, the parent company of *PRIDE*, a local magazine publication distributed in Charlotte, North Carolina, and surrounding areas.

"COMMUNITY PRIDE" was the initial name of the publication when it made its debut in 1993 at *The Charlotte Observer*. Dee worked and excelled in sales for the magazine and later ran the publication there. Some years later, she accepted the offer to purchase the magazine, and in 2001, the first edition of *PRIDE Magazine* was published.

Pride is well-known, well-received and an influential community icon. The printed magazine is polished and well-produced, along with a complimenting digital version. *PRIDE* is full of positive realism and meaningful stories. One of my favorite issues featured the cover story of a Black homeless woman who was educated, not on drugs or any of those typical stereotypes, yet she lost everything after she lost her job. These stories are told on a small scale, but they matter to the larger Black community.

As we discussed earlier in the chapter, magazines nowadays struggle to stay afloat. But Pride's success can be attributed to its subscribership, local advertisers, events, community affairs, and its involvement in the city of Charlotte at large. It also has a nonprofit arm that reaches underserved youth, and its public relations division has helped elevate the brand by providing content and engagement expertise. This valuable service creates opportunities to connect communities of color with corporations, nonprofits, healthcare advocates, and governmental agencies.

Pride Sunset Jazz Festival

While no longer operational, the Pride Sunset Jazz Festival was one of Pride's initial signature events that featured free entertainment. Beyond audiences coming from all parts of the greater Charlotte region, the draw was an opportunity for businesses and sponsors to mingle with the community outside the corporate bounds. Everyone looked forward to the annual weekend of leisure, music and other entertainment. The event drew about six thousand people and was an ideal and typical grassroots way to bridge and build relationships.

Pride Educational Empowerment Program

Founded in 2007, "PEEP," now named the Pride Educational Empowerment Program, is a 501(c)(3) whose initiatives promote education and marketable skills relative to entrepreneurship, wealth creation, and career mentoring.

PEEP's primary emphasis is on helping underserved high school students understand the racial wealth gap and how to generate wealth for themselves, their families, and the community via an eight-week stock market curriculum. Since its inception, PEEP has provided over $100,000 in scholarships to worthy students.

Pride's Signature Event

The Pride Awards continue to be Pride's signature event, recognizing the contributions and achievements of local Black Americans. Each year, the awards focus on a different theme, such as the arts, education, entrepreneurship, and community service. In addition to celebrating the accomplishments of individuals, the Pride Awards recognize and support local nonprofit organizations whose work is significant to African Americans. The event has donated over a quarter of a million dollars to worthy causes.

Lessons from Dee Dixon and PRIDE

In her own words: "I am a mission and vision person. I believe in working from them and changing them as needed." Dee Dixon and PRIDE's apparent mission has been to work from foundational standards of excellence, to recognize and give back to the Black community and the Charlotte community. Understanding the role of relationships and how relatable events galvanize groups to celebrate themselves and their culture collectively have contributed to the perfect formula for PRIDE'S success.

Black Media Is Here to Stay.

Perhaps the sector including Black agencies and Black media will need to find strategic and path-blazing trails to revamp and flourish in the ways it once did. But it's not going anywhere, and neither is its effect on loyal Black consumers. In essence, Black media is like a small business, and there is a large and merited "support small business" movement across this country. Black media isn't excluded in this reach for support.

●

OPPORTUNITIES

The opportunity for leaders and decision-makers in Black and non-Black companies is to:

1. Take an independent approach to ad and media spending. If your target market includes Black consumers, meet with local, regional, and national Black media outlets to strategize and create a plan together to reach your Black consumer segment optimally.

2. Consider using Black agencies to carry out the strategy and implementation for a portion or all of your marketing and advertising efforts.

3. Invest in Black market research data to understand and effectively implement your brand's story using the most influential Black media platforms.

Why not stick with general marketing agencies and general media outlets?

There has to be an interest in genuinely connecting with the Black American consumer. Just because things work well doesn't mean they couldn't work even better.

Black consumers are highly influential spenders. They are loyal advocates for brands, products, and services they believe in. They are just as progressive and worthy as any other demographic in the United States.

Black agencies and Black media personnel aren't second-rate or subpar. They're educated, enterprising, highly creative, and professional individuals. And I think sometimes these attributes are worth repeating. I think they're worth reiterating because blind spots do exist. Unconscious biases are present in the thinking and decision-making of many leaders in these onboarding roles. When you hear and understand, again, that there's no difference in the education, business acumen, professionalism, and creativity between that of a Black advertising executive and a white or other non-Black ad exec, perhaps you'll question why you keep maintaining the status quo—why Black talent and Black media are automatically excluded from your lists of considerations. Maybe you'll come up with an answer that isn't based on long-held beliefs or biases—and that's when you can make a new decision.

●

○   ✖

Potential challenges with Programmatic Ad Buying

Why Black agencies should buy Black Media: Audience Targeting

The Situation

Direct targeting of an ad entails reaching a specific group of consumers who fall within certain demographics and psychographics of that target. For example: "A luxury car manufacturer wants to advertise its newest fleet of vehicles with a $70-thousand or higher price point. The direct targeting filters will be set to only show or broadcast the ad to those whose household income is in the top 10 percent.

The Challenge

Given that Badge Value is essential to Black Americans, how can programmatic buying include this insight?

I recall being in a meeting with several Black agency representatives. The meeting was held by an automobile manufacturer (The Client), who invited the agencies to participate in a pitch for the advertising business of one of their upscale vehicles. The Client took the agencies through the background and other pertinent details related to the assignment. The description of the recommended Black target mirrored the general market audience. When the income specs that included the higher income bracket were presented, the entire room erupted with "No!!" and heads shaking throughout the room with disapproval. Black agencies understand Badge Value and how the Black consumer that otherwise fits the target would likely buy an expensive car first, before a home, regardless of their income.

Badge Value is a wildcard because it cannot be grouped with other traditional target descriptors or numerical values. This is where programmatic algorithms miss the mark.

So, what's the solution?

My intention is to spark these types of conversations all over the nation to find the answers. I guess it will require including some qualitative indicator that doesn't operate in error—missing an entire market of potential buyers.

Notes

1. "Why Black Media Matters Now," The Black Media Initiative: Center for Community Media, Craig Newmark Graduate School of Journalism at the City University of New York, 2021

2. *Geekset Podcast:* The only Podcast that Blends Hip-Hop Culture & Geek Culture in one place. Hosts: Rudy "Young Deuces" Strong, Ron "Bacardi" Cegers, Aderson "Lib" Gonzalez, and Demetrius "Didge" Strong

3. "What Black Twitter Means to The BET Awards," Sesali Bowen, https://www.paramount.com/news/content-and-experiences/what-black-twitter-means-to-the-bet-awards, 6/19/2019

4. "Why Black Media Matters Now," The Black Media Initiative: Center for Community Media, Craig Newmark Graduate School of Journalism at the City University of New York, 2021

5. Cheryl Thompson-Morton, Black Media Initiative Director, Center for Community Media Craig Newmark Graduate School of Journalism at the City University of New York, 10/6/2021

6. Study: "Why Black Media Matters Now," Center for Community Media Craig Newmark Graduate School of Journalism at the City University of New York, Oct. 2021

7. "Cataloging the Black travel experience," Patricia King and Martinique Lewis, *Travel Weekly,* 12/21/21

8. Crain's Chicago Business

9. "African American Media Today," cdn.givingcompass.org

10. "New Habits for Multicultural Growth: P&G chief brand officer Marc Pritchard Shares 5 Essential Habits to Seize the Multicultural Growth Opportunity," ANA Multicultural Marketing & Diversity Conference, 2021 https://us.pg.com/blogs/multicultural-growth/

11. Pride Communications, Inc. is the parent company of *Pride Magazine,* a local publication distributed in Charlotte, N.C., and the surrounding areas.

20

Black Cyberspace Propels Black Culture

As Millennials came of age, Black social media became a widely-used platform that advanced Black culture tremendously. I remember producing a heavily shared infographic in 2013 titled, "Black Twitter: Real and Influential." In it, I shared how Black Twitter users were ushering in a new movement and how Black Millennials were likely to follow one another on the platform, to affirm their beliefs and spark interpersonal conversations. I included statistics like 28 percent of adult African Americans tweeted, compared to 12 percent non-Hispanic whites and 14 percent Hispanics, as well as the fact that even when Black Twitter was first established, it already had a Wikipedia page that chronicled its history, influence and credibility. What was happening in Black cyberspace, was eye-opening. They were building a cybercommunity to connect and propel interests and issues that mattered to them.

Later, Jason Parham would write for Wired.com that "Black Twitter has become the most dynamic subset not only of Twitter but of the wider social internet." It is not a stand-alone platform influenced by Black people. It is a collective of several different communities of predominantly Black people.

Parham wrote, it is "capable of creating, shaping, and remixing popular culture at light speed, it remains the incubator of nearly every meme, hashtag and social-justice cause worth knowing about. It is both news and analysis, call and response, judge and jury—a comedy showcase, therapy session, and family cookout all in one. Black Twitter is a multiverse, simultaneously an archive and an all-seeing lens into the future."

Breaking News and Empowering People

Black Twitter heavily shaped how and when pressing social-justice issues surfaced in the Black community when major local and cable news networks underreported. And it helped many of these political and grassroots brand movements reach Black communities with speed and distance. Further, Black Twitter proved to be where social experiments and kitchen-table conversations influenced trends in a major way. As they share and exchange information like fashion tips, recipes, music, and other popular subjects of interest, big brands have been known to watch and take notes—showcasing some of those same trends in their campaigns.

Black Twitter also has the power to call out brands and situations that have been proven less favorably to the Black community: A juror from the George Zimmerman trial lost a tell-all book deal, and Paula Dean lost her TV show after Black Twitter alerted the public about her past use of racial slurs. Dove, Gucci, and H&M have all felt the pain of being trolled on the internet for weeks by Black Twitter after featuring Blacks in negative, stereotypical advertising.

Black Twitter was the beginning. The momentum of that platform sparked how Black people used and influenced other platforms, like Clubhouse, Instagram, and TikTok. "Black" added to the descriptions of these platforms indicates "Black community," not a place. Today, Black Gen Z content creators heavily influence TikTok and YouTube, and there has been resounding pushback by a cyberspace phenomenon: the non-credited use of Black creators' content.

Countless reports and online protests call for non-Black users who copy or otherwise steal original Black content to give proper credit to its owner. Jalaiah Harmon, a Black teenager from greater Atlanta, created a dance—called "Renegade" on TikTok.

Addison Rae Easterling and Charli D'Ameilo, two of the most popular people on TikTok, copied the dance and labeled themselves as the creators. After the dance went viral, Addison and Charli were invited to perform it on Jimmy Fallon's *Tonight Show*.[1] When Easterling reportedly performed "sluggish, watered down versions" of Renegade and other dances created by other Black dance influencers, Black Twitter and Black TikTok especially, began posting the original dance alongside Easterling's version. It became a big story and lead to Black content creators calling for a boycott of these platforms.

Eventually, Jalaiah, Charli, and Addison received an invitation from the NBA, where they were offered prime seats to one of the games and the opportunity to dance the TikTok dance with the players and cheerleaders. Jimmy Fallon also invited them to perform on his show.

This is just one example of how many Black creators' work is stolen and capitalized by white viewers in social media.

White and non-Black users and influencers have been given million-dollar brand endorsements and deals, as well as TV appearances, based on a viral video that they copied from Black content creators. The Black community comes together to hold these platforms accountable in cyberspace, as well as in the real world. All in all, these digital communities give Black people a unique space to achieve connectedness, realize ideas and dreams, and push Black culture forward. Understanding the multipurpose uses in which Blacks engage with technology, comes from first understanding their ability to creatively engineer various digital platforms and tools, to establish community and communication in cyberspace.

Note
1. "Addison Rae *Tonight Show* Appearance Sparks a Conversation About Race, Crediting Creators and Bias on Social Media," Paige Skinner, lamag.com, 3/30/2021

21

Black Representation in Market Research

Portraying Black Excellence is Paramount— Where's the Designated Black Consumer Market Research?

"Qualitative research should be non-fact-finding but ensure a positive experience." —Emily Spensieri, president & brand strategist, HerBrand Consulting

Black Respondents Are Different from Mainstream Respondents; thus, Relevant Research Practices Matter

The market research industry shamefully lacks diversity and inclusivity. Black and brown people are scarce in the industry. According to Media Post,[1] the breakout of race and ethnic representation in the market research industry is as follows:

- 68.9% White
- 13.2% Asian
- 10.2% Latino
- 4.9% Black American
- 0.2% American Indian & Alaska Native

The lack of representation underscores how market research is not fully contributing to the marketing and market research industries and society, due to the deficit of insights. Diverse talent, relevant tools, and practices would direct recruiting and interviewing of underserved segments and help brands understand and better communicate with them. Thus, business leaders must unlearn those one-dimensional traditional practices to fix the deficit and incorporate a new approach.

I am grateful for the clients who invest in Black studies and the respondents who participate in them. Yet, comparatively speaking of the industry at large, throughout my market research career, there has been little designated research conducted with Black Americans by Black Americans.

Most of my work has been conducting qualitative research—focus groups, ethnographies, one-on-ones, executive interviews, listening sessions, and the like with Black Americans. What I love about my work is the opportunity to converse with respondents—real people—who, in addition to sharing their opinions about particular products, services, or advertising, talk about their dreams, hopes, experiences, and challenges as Black Americans. I've learned so much about the Black community and myself from these conversations. I live in a Black community in Chicago and appreciate how daily interactions with the Black community have served as "my lab" for observations. But it's the research projects, combined with my personal experience, that has been a major resource of Black insights for my work over the years.

Today, some major big-spender brands are moving away from focus groups. The quest for Black (and any) insights from this methodology has become questionable. They believe little is achieved from the process and say they aren't learning anything new.

Here's the problem. In today's culture, where diversity has become one of the drivers for inclusion, for market research, diversity is meant to cover a variety of ethnic homogeneous studies. But that rarely happens. Very few brands are investing in Black-designated research. They pat themselves on the back for practicing "fair representation" by including one or two Black people in predominantly white focus groups and look to Census population numbers as their rationale—If Blacks are 14 percent of the population, then 14 percent should be represented in a mainstream focus group. Again, *"They speak English don't they?"* is a rationale for not investing in Black research and, therefore, rolling Black respondents in with mainstream. Many Black respondents in this situation are less honest and authentic. They tend to tell the truth but not always the whole truth.

Don't Underestimate the Power of the Introduction.

More than 20 years ago, when conducting focus groups in some of the top Black populated markets, a few respondents from various markets stopped to chat with me before exiting the focus group room:

> **Why the all-Black Group?** *Why are they separating us from everyone else? I wanted to share something about being Black (in America), but I wasn't sure what was happening.*

Black people *should be* comfortable in focus group settings, especially with a Black moderator. But they aren't always comfortable. Given our history, it's common for Black people to be suspicious. Consider the Black focus group experience, whether in person or virtually . . .

- They are likely screened and recruited by a white recruiter.

- They are likely to be greeted by a white hostess.

- Most are not "virgin" respondents and believe those observing are white.

So, the revelation of the exit questions from Black respondents years ago inspired me to invite Black respondents to be . . . *Black.* In every group since then, during the introduction, I ask: "How many have participated in a focus group discussion—virtually or in person?" Hands go up. I then ask, "How many have participated in an all-Black group?" Maybe one hand, of 6 to 8 respondents is raised, but most often, none.

I then explain that sharing their honest opinions helps brands better understand and serve the Black community. Thus, it is essential for them to share their honest perspectives from the Black lens and to be authentic during this discussion. "Think about Thanksgiving," I would say, "and how some of us have moved from the formal dining room table to the kitchen to have dessert, which might be . . ." I pause, and many shout out: "sweet potato pie, banana pudding, pound cake, etc."

I continue with . . . "So when it's just us, sitting around the table having our favorite dessert. I want to have that conversation here!"

None of this is leading. Blackness and Black culture are on our radar every day. Most Black people think about Blackness 90 percent of the time, *vs.* whites who think about being white 10 percent of the time. So in research, especially in this industry that lacks racial diversity, it's important to make respondents feel comfortable by introducing relevant and relatable examples in the methodology.

Black Interviewers Matter

Non-Black interviewers can have conversations with Black respondents in qualitative research studies, but Black interviewers create a better connection and encourage honest conversations.

Recently, my company conducted focus groups for a major drugstore chain. Included in that study were separate groups of Black men. I hired a Black male moderator to run the virtual groups. The men were ecstatic over his presence. Following introductions, the moderator allowed them a few minutes to express their delight in participating in an all-Black male focus group with a Black male moderator . . .

"This is really cool!"

"I never expected to see all these brothers and a brother leading the discussion! No offense, man, I just knew you were going to be white."

"No one ever asks for our opinion."

More comments like these were shared, and similar comments from previous mixed-gender groups are often heard as well.

For non-Black interviewers addressing an all-Black group, it's important to begin by addressing the elephant in the room. Tell "your" truth; be honest and authentic:

I'm ＿＿＿ (white, Asian, etc.). I am not going to pretend that I fully understand Black culture . . .

Then encourage respondents to "tell their truth." Invite Black respondents to be authentically "Black." Help respondents understand why their honest opinions matter.

Biased Beginnings:
Automated Information and Artificial Intelligence

I welcome progress driven by technology, even in the face of machines replacing humans.

I'm not a fan of people losing their livelihood to technology, yet, I, too, enjoy the convenience of an ATM, digital reserve parking lot spaces, toll passes, etc. It's progress. It's where we have evolved.

Market research is evolving, too—to automated information data and artificial intelligence. Automated information and artificial intelligence in market research are designed to streamline the research process and make it more efficient and time-saving.

Some of these benefits include using time more efficiently and measuring results more accurately. Improving technology also allows researchers to tap into unused resources and discover new opportunities. Other benefits include managing remote workers more easily and reducing the use of paper.

It's great to have a program that captures words and phrases from focus group recordings, organizes them into similar categories, and tabulates them—versus listening to them, and manually performing the tabulations—what a time saver!

The Problem? Biased Information is often Baked into
AI Methodologies.

Everyone has biases, and people embed their biases into technology. An algorithm is a procedure used for solving a problem or performing a computation. Algorithms act as an exact list of instructions that conduct specified actions step by step in either hardware- or software-based routines.[2] Automated intelligence and algorithms as related to market research are often developed from standards and experiences by non-diverse engineers, programmers, coders, and technicians. Their biases and misunderstanding of Black culture can lead to information that promotes stereotypes, which would continue to widen the gap of ethnic understanding, connectivity, and intersectionality.

Because language is the cultural identifier, as mentioned in Chapter Five, some words or expressions used by Black people may be misconstrued by non-Black analysts. For example, during a focus group discussion with Black men, they often used the word "dog" or "dawg" to address or describe a buddy or close male friend. An automated information program captured this expression and organized it as a situation for a veterinarian or a negative expression about Black men born out of the Black community. Non-Black analysts were ready to report the findings as delivered and incorrectly.

Artificial intelligence prioritizes user preference, while our civil rights laws prioritize equality of opportunity.[3] In the 2020 film documentary *Coded Bias,* then Massachusetts Information Technology student and Ph.D. candidate, Joy Buolamwini shares her experience with artificial intelligence and facial recognition programs.

Joy decided to build the "Aspire Mirror" as one of her class projects. The mirror would be an inspirational tool to motivate her, especially in the morning before she started her day. It could include various images of animals or people that she could transpose over an image of her face. She chose an image of Serena Williams and used computer vision software to create the mirror. It didn't work. Well, it didn't work for her dark skin. Her face was not detected. So, Joy put on a white mask and the software detected her face. When she took off the white mask, there was no detection. Joy checked the lighting and camera position. Still the same results without the white mask. During further investigation of the program, she learned that most faces in the program's database were of men, lighter skin individuals, and not faces like hers—darker skin, with a broader nose, and full lips.

Hollywood creates stories about machines that not only think but reason. And while we look at these stories as entertainment and pure fiction, there is more truth baked into these themes than we realize.

The *Journal of the American Medical Informatics Association* suggests, that if those models use data that reflect existing racial bias in healthcare delivery, AI that was meant to benefit all patients may worsen healthcare disparities for people of color. While the sophisticated technology may be new, the FTC's attention to automated decision making is not. The FTC has decades of experience enforcing three laws important to developers and users of AI:[4]

Section 5 of the FTC Act. The FTC Act prohibits unfair or deceptive practices. That would include the sale or use of, for example, racially biased algorithms.

Fair Credit Reporting Act. The FCRA comes into play in certain circumstances where an algorithm is used to deny people employment, housing, credit, insurance, or other benefits.

Equal Credit Opportunity Act. The ECOA makes it illegal for a company to use a biased algorithm that results in credit discrimination on the basis of race, color, religion, national origin, sex, marital status, age, or because a person receives public assistance.

We have to approach this new world of technological market research with both enthusiasm and caution. As business leaders and market researchers we must be vigilant about planning, foresight and inclusion. In particular, we must determine how the market research industry can harness the benefits of AI (and traditional market research practices) without inadvertently introducing bias or other unfair outcomes.

We must ensure that Blacks and other people of color are at the table and their ideas and voices are welcomed through their respective cultural experiences. These collective ideas would surely be useful in creating programs, methodologies and tools to ensure a broader reach, effective participation and insightful analysis in our studies.

Relevant market research matters!

○   ✖

Market Research Needs (More) Black Anthropologists

The desire for understanding "why" about anything and everything has always been with me. I never outgrew asking why from my childhood. It has been the impetus for passionately delivering to brands and society insights for better understanding and engagement with Black America. It has also fueled my love for anthropology and anthropologists.

A simple definition of anthropology according to the American Anthropological Association is: Anthropology is the study of what makes us human. There are four subfields of anthropology: archaeology, biological anthropology, cultural anthropology, and linguistic anthropology. The latter two are practiced most in market research.

> **Sociocultural anthropologists** explore how people in different places live and understand the world around them. They want to know what people think is important and the rules they make about how they should interact with one another.

> **Linguistic anthropologists** study the many ways people communicate across the globe. They are interested in how language is linked to how we see the world and how we relate to each other.[5]

I embrace all of these definitions. They fit nicely into the wheelhouse of my work.

In 2022, I had the opportunity to hear a discussion about market research, anthropology and Black Americans. It was an online fireside chat hosted by OverIndex, a community dedicated to building strong Black professional leaders in Market Research and Strategy, while tackling systematic issues in the industry. I am the Executive Sponsor of Overindex. Our guest was Autumn McDonald, the CEO of ADM Strategy, and a sociocultural anthropologist and insights maven.

Autumn brings years of national and global research to the table and a Master of Science degree in Applied Anthropology from the University of North Texas. Her specialization is Socio-Cultural Anthropology, with an emphasis in intersections of race, ethnicity, and space.

She was interviewed by Alexandrea Davis and Erica Williams-London, founders of OverIndex. Autumn blew us away with astute insights about the practice of anthropology in general and the benefits of using it to answer the "why" question as it relates to Black Americans. Here are some of the highlights from that discussion:

OverIndex: How is anthropology used in the market research space?

McDonald: Anthropologists do some of the same research projects as market researchers. We just approach them differently. We always strive to uncover "the why" behind the what. We tend to spend more time in the field with subjects. Where an ethnography can last 30 minutes to a few hours shopping with subjects or in their homes or restaurants, an anthropological study can last for months or years with constituents.

We go through pages and pages of extremely detailed field notes. We analyze these field notes, often coding them by every single phrase. And as we're coding, we're creating quantitative hierarchies in which we are looking for different cultural dynamics—balances of power, positions of privilege— all kinds of themes that we can use to say, this is a cultural context, a social context, an emotional context, and use these to empower our clients.

Anthropology helps us understand what is meaningful and helps make the invisible visible. It harnesses the meanings that are present in symbols, products, services, life experiences, and human reactions. It helps us elicit a deeper understanding of the human experience; provides a human-centric perspective by uncovering social, cultural, and emotional contexts not provided by market research alone.

OverIndex: What is the importance of anthropology in market research especially with the Black population?

McDonald: Anthropology helps us know our (Black) selves better. It helps us understand why Black Americans do what they do; it identifies and uncovers the cultural underpinnings.

Anthropology humanizes Blackness and Black people in other types of research. It helps combat the oversimplification of Blackness especially in the way big brands and large research companies design their research— and how they approach their marketing communications.

Anthropology has provided frameworks for understanding how capitalism affects Black people. It calls out privilege and replaces the biased questioning—from being "What's wrong with them?" to "Why am I, like, the way I am?"

Notes

1. "Lack of Diversity in Market Research: What Can We Do?", Scott McDonald, Mediapost, 9/17/2021

2. techtarget.com

3. "Artificial Intelligence: How the internet gatekeeper can affect your civil rights," Lindsey Nako, Impactfund.org, 3/1/2020

4. "Aiming for truth, fairness, and equity in your company's use of AI," Elisa Jillson, *Business Blog*, FTC.gov, 4/19/2021

5. American Anthropological Association

PART FIVE

How to Win Black Loyalty

Brands that Win Center the Black Experience, Consistently

Companies and brands are increasingly entering the diversity conversation with a desire to connect with Black and POC audiences. Unfortunately, many just don't know where to start. For example, what story should be told? It's even pertinent for some decision-makers to hash out how far they can and should align with Black consumers without risking losing their base mainstream consumer. As such, sometimes the desire to connect doesn't advance past the idea to connect. Sometimes, it only goes as far as a conversation or a brief market study. Other times an idea or initiative that has been researched, vetted, and formed into a great ad campaign reaches the market. It turns out to be a great success, and then . . . *nothing*. Consumers never see or experience another inclusive campaign or offering from that brand again. What's up with that?

Often, as a market researcher, I survey the latest local and national campaigns. I take note of the overall progress in the advertising and marketing industry, and I especially examine the working parts of the campaigns that make a splash within the Black consumer community. These are the campaigns being tweeted, re-shared and highlighted in articles because they are fresh and so against the grain. It is my wish that one day, inclusive, Black-talent-led national campaigns are so commonplace, that it's no longer news. But while it is, I'll be the first to admit that one-off ad wins barely move the gauge on the trust-factor scale. Black Americans welcome the representation that we so longingly demand, and are excited to see it when the consumer brands that we buy into show us in a positive, progressive light. However, that excitement is almost simultaneously met with skepticism. Why? Let's be honest. Brands that market these consumer products aren't doing so out of pure altruism.

This is about consumer dollars. Consumers want to feel understood. And good campaigns accomplish both: They tap into the psychology of those consumers—who they are and what they want; and they rake in the coins.

An impressive campaign that is, what I like to call, Black-positive-approved because it consists of campaign messaging that incorporates positive messaging, prominent Black presence and includes Black talent or leadership behind the scenes. Those are the ingredients to achieving a winning campaign that gets the attention of Black consumers.

When a campaign launches locally or across the country with all of those elements, Black people certainly take notice! They celebrate that win. But for brands who bring the message for the first time, Black consumers are bound to question their motive. The mindset behind this reluctance:

"Are they only after my money? Or, do they care about me and the things important to me?"

There have been countless examples throughout Black American history, where Black endorsement was essential to winning or gaining something, and thus leveraged by "the other." The painful problem however, is that leverage is almost always purely for the benefit of "the other," while almost intentionally leaving the Black community itself in the dust.

There's Warranted Cynicism

It's common to see a campaign targeting Black consumers, in all the right ways, turn out to make big missteps with the Black consumer. Although Walmart has been a brand that for years has invested in Black marketing, Black agencies, Black advertising, Black research and Black media, in 2022, the company found itself under scrutiny for using known Black phrases and colloquialisms on candles and ice cream during Juneteenth and other public holidays that would attract Black buyers. Bath and Body Works was under the microscope for African, and African American-related, designs on their products during Black History Month.

Black consumers wanted to know who was behind the designs and if any Black creatives or leaders were being credited. As mentioned in Chapter Five's Insight and Opportunity section, language is important; however, campaigns cannot slap phrases on products and expect Black consumers to feel included.

Ultimately, Black people want to see and experience that Black APRR (Authentic, Positivity, Realism, and Representation) that we discussed in previous chapters—and they want to experience it consistently.

It's important that Black consumers trust the brands they buy into. They trust brands because there is a proven, consistent culture of authenticity, positivity and representation. One feel-good campaign won't earn that trust. But . . . It's a start.

I've started to ease my criticism—*only a bit*—when it comes to recognizing the first wins and intermittent efforts brands put out there. I believe a positive and progressive mindset about how brands are trying to close the gap, matters in encouraging them to continue trying to close the gap. To brand leaders and decision makers: Well-researched, targeted campaigns work! They resonate. They matter.

Keep doing it.

In this section, I provide two examples: one is a past and ongoing win (P&G) and the other is an impactful first win (Pixar). We will examine the elements that made those wins successful. These elements are great tools to observe, and most can be added to your strategies for effective research, development, and marketing to Black consumers (and People of Color).

Let me explain how to do it right . . .

22

Characteristics of a
Winning Brand

Under a watchful eye, Black consumers nowadays are careful about where and how they spend their hard-earned dollars. Today more than ever, they have a multitude of choices at their fingertips and they're aware of their consumer power. Thanks to social media and online shopping, as well as the rise of Black owned businesses, traditional big brands have significant competition and must keep up, if they want to win.

"Who's winning and who's getting it right?" are questions clients and colleagues frequently ask me. Ideally, in a fair and equitable marketing industry every brand and organization would be interested in winning Black consumers' loyalty. In reality, the level of involvement some decision-makers commit to is limited to checking a box on a few requirements.

As I write this book, in my estimation, no one is getting it right—not on a measurable acceptable basis. After years of working in the multicultural and Black market-research sectors, I have identified some core requirements for earning that "winning" badge with these deserving consumers. Walmart, Toyota, Procter & Gamble Corporate, and McDonald's have years of consistent relationships with Black agencies, and Black media, and come closest to what I consider the following nine essential criteria for getting consumers' attention and then getting them to like, share, follow and buy brands of their choice.

1. Understand, to some extent, the Black historical lens.

Change your mindset. This means giving pause to personal beliefs, biases, and perspectives about Black Americans and learning to interject empathy (not excuses) in your thought process to see things, from Black Americans' perspective.

2. Present strong, clear messaging and visual portrayals.

Communications must sound and feel authentically and unapologetically Black—Think 4C hair and curvy, dark-skinned women in a Dove commercial.

3. Consistent inclusion at all touch points.

One-off wins are not wins. While a resonant campaign may generate temporary buzz, it generally will be short-lived. For Black consumers to not only buy, but share and become advocates for your brand, they want to see themselves portrayed positively in your brand campaigns, they want to be included in social media conversations, and they want to know there is a vested interest in Black. Consistency is key.

Netflix hired a team of savvy Black senior level professionals and influencers who took the reins and connected with Black subscribers globally. Their segment of the Netflix brand was called "Strong Black Lead" and for a time, they captured Black consumers in a winning way. As of the writing of this book, they've dismantled their Black consumer and multicultural segmentation efforts.

4. Tell a story.

Anyone can come up with a catchphrase and anyone can get in on a hashtag. But telling a story involves an understanding of one's world. When P&G created a series of commercials that spoke to what it's like to be Black, they had a win.

5. Consistent Black APRR.

Everyone notices when Black men, women and children are portrayed in a fun, positive and endearing light. It stands out because Black people are typically portrayed in the media, in less than positive ways. When campaigns use authenticity, positivity, relatability, and representation to accurately show a loving Black mother, a devoted Black husband and intelligent Black children, Black consumers lean in, they share it, and it puts your brand on their radar. The importance here is consistently showing them in this positive light.

6. Invest for the long term, with Black agency partners.

These firms have extensive expertise with the Black American consumer market. Their specialization includes: advertising and communications, market research, digital marketing, public relations, media buying, consulting firms, talent agencies, etc.

7. Recurring investment in designated Black research.

Qualitative research can provide an opportunity to connect with this segment, and observe their opinions and perspectives—in their words, in their spaces, and in environments that are most comfortable for them. **Quantitative research** provides the measurement of demographics, attitudes and behaviors. It's not either or, but both.

8. Invest in Black media.

Black media, especially Black owned and operated media, are the conduit to the Black community.

9. Be an Ally.

With issues from police brutality to political and corporate disenfranchisement, Black consumers are looking to align with brands that are allies, taking a stand with them and speaking up about issues that matter. When Rihanna accepted an NAACP Image award in 2020, she said this:

"How many of us . . . have friends and colleagues and partners and friends from other races, sexes, religions—they want to break bread with you, right? They like you! Well then this is their problem, too. So when we're marching, and protesting and posting about the Michael Brown Juniors and the Atatiana Jeffersons of the world, tell your friends to pull up."

"Pull up" means to stand with us, for us, do what you can—rather than sitting on the sidelines and observing—and be an ally.

23

When Brands Get It Right

The Procter & Gamble Effect:
Demonstrating Allyship by Telling a Different Story

Like many households, you will find a number of P&G brands in my home. Crest, Tide, Bounce, Aussie, Gillette, Bounty, and Charmin have been staples for years.

From an industry perspective, I've had much respect for P&G as a corporate brand for investing in and having long-term relationships (for decades) with Black consumers and Black agency partners. Within the past 10 years, my appreciation has grown for P&G corporate for their fight against racism and telling the unbridled truth about the full Black experience, as one of their tactics to end racism.

P&G Plants the Seeds for Change

As the world's largest packaged goods conglomerate, P&G has the resources to reach hundreds of millions of diverse consumers all over the world, with an abundance of product offerings. With this massive reach and global brand presence, I have observed an equally massive commitment, at the corporate level, to be allies for underserved markets and, in their own way, take steps to combat systemic racism. I have yet to see another company match P&G's global efforts in a way that I believe will lead to change.

P&G's attentiveness to tell stories that rarely get told became more apparent to me when they rolled out "Nostalgic Dad," an award-winning Tide-with-Downy television commercial, created by Burrell Communications. It featured a Black father comforting his young son, as the child slept on his chest. Both characters were clad in crisp white t-shirts and the feeling of the moment in this TV spot was that "all was right" in the world. We tested the spot in separate groups of Black and white female heads of households. The white women received the overall message as: "Tide gets clothes clean." The Black women received the same message, but also responded with extreme excitement over a different additional message, which was not on the white respondents' radar. For Black women, seeing a Black man in a big-brand-name commercial, showing up as a responsible, caring father, was a demonstration of respect. On a national stage, it showed the men in their lives the way *they* see them, too.

That was in 2005. The commercial ran in the general market as well as Black media and won several awards. I consider that commercial a classic. It was unprecedented during the time due to the overwhelming positive response, which laid the foundation, I believe, for P&G to tell more stories like this about Black America. Black women had such a resoundingly positive reaction to the ad, it nudged P&G to look deeper into what made them respond that way.

Here's why Black research at P&G mattered.

In 2006, a group of visionary Black women launched *My Black is Beautiful,* a community-based platform created to empower, celebrate and ignite meaningful dialogue on the subject of Black beauty. In addition to pop-culture and beauty topics for readers, space dedicated to bias, societal standards in beauty, as well as Black beauty's influence on mainstream culture sparked lots of conversation. *My Black Is Beautiful* stood out for being a platform specifically for Black women and Black beauty culture.

In 2019, the platform expanded from an initiative to a brand, launching a haircare collection. Black women were behind the collection, incorporating a unique understanding of the intricacies of Black haircare—a category sorely overlooked in the mainstream beauty market. By tapping into Black haircare desires and needs, they were able to capture a loyal consumer base.[1]

Stepping Up: Not Just Talking About It—Being About It.

Fighting racism is included in P&G's corporate brand objectives

In 2016 P&G CEO David Taylor and Marc Pritchard, P&G's chief brand officer hosted an internal event for over 500 brand managers and directors: *Stepping UP to the African American Market* while also celebrating the tenth anniversary of *My Black is Beautiful.* The affair was enjoyable and packed a serious punch in terms of keeping the objective central and on point. P&G representatives, nationally renowned journalist Soledad O'Brien, and I presented keynotes and videos that emphasized the importance of investing in the Black consumer. Today, Pritchard continues to inspire the industry to follow his lead in breaking down the barriers of racism. You can find a blog on P&G's corporate website "Take on Race," where they pledge to:

". . . create a company and a world where equality and inclusion is the reality for everyone. While this has long been our goal, we're stepping up our efforts to do even more to make this a reality."

Additionally, he and an internal team of executives created an initiative, *Widen the Screen for Diverse Storytelling.* The objective of the initiative includes storytelling through video that portrays the full experience of Black life in America (*see side bar, page 223*). The videos are like movie shorts, each with a distinctive script, storyline, setting and characters who play the role of the real, or ideal, Black experience. You can find the shorts on P&G's corporate website, as well as their social-media platforms. Pritchard shares these shorts, as do I, at many C-suite conferences as a way to show the value of Black consumers using a high-quality, well-produced medium. The hope is to spark much needed conversation around race and inclusion and challenge blind spots and biases.

In another notable mission, Pritchard publicly pledged to set P&G's weekly goal to reach 80 to 90 percent of multicultural consumers. For the Black consumer marketing industry, that requires making substantial investments in Black-owned and Black-operated media, including prominent Black media brands like BET, TVOne, and Revolt.

All along the way, P&G and its leadership has been walking the talk and planting seeds of information and truth. Winning has taken on a bigger broader purpose for this brand. Their actions, allyship and initiatives are having and will continue to make a significant impact. Ultimately, winning comes through shifting mindsets of both leaders and consumers—to build a better industry, better relationships, and a better country.

P&G Takes a Stand

P&G tells the unbridled truth about America's treatment and misperceptions of Black America in three compelling digital shorts

The Talk

Generations of mothers having the required conversation with their children about race and racism against Black people.

The Look

As part of their commitment to diversity and inclusion, P&G created *The Look,* a short film that helps shed light on and continue the conversation about racial bias. In the film, viewers follow a Black man as he moves through different experiences, witnessing the "looks" he gets as he walks his son to school, eats lunch, and goes shopping. These looks demonstrate a barrier to acceptance based on the color of his skin. This man is just one of many people who encounter bias every single day.

Widen the Screen (To widen our view)

The video is from P&G's campaign and platform under the same name to tell stories that represent the full Black experience. In this video viewers are shown partial scenes of Black people in situations where potential stereotypes can be perceived. The announcer in the video goes on to ask: *"If you think you know what's going to happen next, ask yourself why . . ."* and challenges viewers to see more by revealing normal positive outcomes that happen every day in the Black experience.

Note
1. MBIB.com

24

Celebrating First Wins

Pixar, Cultural Trust and Positive Realism in Action

Soul is Pixar's first animated feature centered on a Black protagonist, played by Jamie Foxx, alongside a host of other notable A-list actors and actresses. Another animated Disney film, *Princess and the Frog,* premiered in 2009, featuring a Black princess, the first Black Disney princess in Walt Disney Animation Studio history which was founded in 1923. Heavy criticism ensued, however, due to Princess Tiana (voiced by Anika Noni Rose) not appearing as a princess throughout the movie. Instead, for three-fourths of the film, she was a frog. While the story is the story, is this Positive Realism?

Likewise, *Soul* was praised for its lead character, a Black male music teacher with dreams of being a performing musician, as well as for its incredibly authentic supporting cast. The writing of this film not only included a Black lead, but a glimpse into everything that made his life, Black—Black friends, family and colleagues; Black spaces and environments, as well as important nuances that made his world *real.* For example, there was his overprotective Black mother, who made glances, and uttered phrases that sounded like a Black mother. The leader of the jazz band, Doreatha Williams was a no-nonsense jazz musician, voluptuous, full lips, wide nose, and afro. She was precise, prompt and uncompromising about the excellence of her band's rehearsal time and musicianship. That rigid attitude, for most viewers, would be a reason to categorize her as a Black woman with an attitude—in a derogatory way; or an angry Black woman. Instead, she was passionate about her band, and music, and doing it right. There are many other examples throughout the film, particularly the barbershop scenes, that got my attention, and turned out to be a definite win for Pixar.

Let's explore the man behind this shining example of Black APRR that, in my opinion, made Pixar's *Soul* successful—Kemp Powers, the first African American to co-direct a Disney animated feature. He is a screenwriter and playwright (most notably for *Star Trek: Discovery* and the play *One Night in Miami)*, and he originally joined the *Soul* production team as a writer.

In a mini-documentary series, *Inside Pixar, Inspired: Kemp Powers, Writing Something Real,* Powers discusses his inspiring journey through co-writing and eventually co-directing *Soul:*

> *"Soul* is a really . . . personal and a bit of a dream project for me. The lead in this film is a Black man who's about my age, who's from New York like me, who is also a jazz musician, and I love jazz music. There were lots of elements of this world that I understood pretty thoroughly.
>
> The film had already been in development for several years before I came on board. So there was a certain element of jumping onto a fast-moving train.
>
> I've never collaborated with so many different people. You have to really believe in the spirit of collaboration. Writing on an animated film means having to come up with worlds and characters that feel real. When I started, the main character had already been developed to an extent. But he didn't feel real yet. We kept asking ourselves "what was missing about Joe and how do we make him feel authentically more African American?" At the same time that you're telling a story for everyone, you want to make sure the people from these specific worlds see it as authentic and I just wanted to recognize Joe as Black. There's a scene where Joe gets this big opportunity to perform, he gets a special suit—his gig suit. But as a Black man, it didn't feel right to me that he would be getting ready for his big day,

and not also get his haircut. Based on the design that we had for Joe, I kept thinking, "this guy needs a haircut 'cause it kind of looks a mess. He should be concerned about getting that hair fixed, even just 'lined up.'" The answer was right in front of our face: Joe had to get his hair fixed, and enter a truly Black space and there's no more authentic [of a] Black space in the community than a barbershop. I reached out to the director, Pete Docter, explaining how important it would be for him to get a haircut, and how important it would be to see a Black barbershop in this particular film.

Your barber, in many cases, is the person you have the longest continuing relationship with, outside of your spouse or children. It's hard to find a barber you're comfortable with, so when you find your guy, you really stick with him. The Black barbershop is like the town center of the community. You can go to your average Black barbershop and there will be a Black doctor or lawyer waiting to get his hair cut, after an actor or garbage man. When we're in the shop, we're all the same. Even if you feel like a small person and the world doesn't respect you or treat you right, in the barbershop you have worth, your opinion matters. When you're in the chair for twenty minutes, you're king.

To deal with this culturally specific stuff, Pixar created an Internal Culture Trust, which is made up of Black Pixar employees and an External Culture Trust, which is experts on Black representation in the arts. But one of the challenges of bringing ten Black people into a room and saying, "Okay, what does it mean to be Black?" you're going to get ten different answers. There's no one Black story. I'm trying to tell a story that is authentic, but by no means do I represent everyone. The barbershop scene came from this very personal place as a Black man. But then it was a job to execute it in a way so that it makes sense.

There was some resistance in the beginning to adding a new scene that would require new characters and a new set. The question was, *"Why do we need this?"* When we screened the first draft of the barbershop scene, everyone locked in on it [because] that moment feels so real and authentic. Once they saw the benefit of that, it opened the floodgates to adding authenticity to Joe's character throughout the entire film. I told [the director], "The idea of seeing rendered Black hair of different styles being cut in a Black barbershop, is almost tear-inducing." To have the Pixar animators bring that level of detail to something that is so multifaceted as Black hair of different textures and types, it could be mind-blowing.

This is the first Pixar film that is set in communities and worlds that are African American. [As a writer, director] you feel like this is your story you're putting up on screen, and you want your story told right.

The Value of Black Leadership at the Table and the Big Idea of Cultural Trusts

This film was a first win for Pixar for several reasons, such as the animators' meticulous attention to detail in the rendering of the character's textured hair, physical features and even glances or smirks. All those things feel good to see on the big screen. But from a business and leadership perspective, I want to call out the innovative utilization of cultural trusts. Without the experience and creative input from Black leadership, it's impossible to tell authentic Black stories—in film or in campaigns. The input of Black leadership is invaluable because of their inherent Black lens. Simply put, other people just can't see what we see, and how we see it. There are layers of nuances, histories and perspectives that, if one were to blink, they'd miss it. I'm willing to bet that's why we see so many marketing blunders. Non-Black creative leads oftentimes miss what a Black decision maker would immediately catch. Pixar not only got their Black staff involved, they created an external group of experts made up of musicians, artists, professors and authors who could offer insights and provide feedback on the storyline, screening and overall progress. This is a first win for me, because it demonstrates Black value from beginning to end, behind the scenes and on the big screen.

PART SIX

So What? Now What?

Closing Thoughts

We, as human beings, are often quick to judge, in a negative way, people or situations that are different from those that are familiar to us. The human brain evaluates everything we experience and rejects most new or different things to protect us from threats and danger and preserve our way of being. If we were to take a moment, take a breath, and challenge ourselves with more thoughtful questions, we can tap into the intellectual curiosity that I believe we are all born with but don't always use.

Our intelligence—our ability to reason, redefine and reimagine ourselves, others, and experiences could be instrumental to our survival. If we didn't have this intelligence, we'd remain in a state of judgment too long and persistently reject everything different from our norm—likely leading to instability and the collapse of our collective human journey.

Reasoning is all about asking the question "why."

In the world of growing diverse populations, asking why is also critical for business leaders and the everyday person. Whether you are building strategies for consumer engagement or a neighbor living in a diverse community, asking why is likely the single most crucial question to ask yourself that would help you find answers to questions around differences, and provide you with the foundation for planning your next steps.

Let me explain . . .

25

Begin with "Why"

Asking "why" leads one to depart from their own norm and go on a quest, seeking new and promising experiences.

Concerning the Black experience in America, we've been asking why for a very long time, and we've even done the work to develop complex answers. Never before in our history have we had such vast vocabulary and language to define and explain the conditions we face and the reasons for them.

A dear friend and colleague, Victoria Lynn Childress, observes race globally on her multifarious travels and excursions. With traveling as her "way of life" for nearly two decades, she explained her experience in a conversation with me:

I've had many conversations about race with many friends across a few different continents. They ask me "why" when they see armored police standing ground among peaceful protestors, or even why I've chosen to leave the U.S. and emigrate to another country. I know my personal reasons, but I struggle to be able to satisfactorily answer why things are the way they are in America. In fact, I often tell them, "we're still trying to figure it out."

The race condition in the United States is precarious from the general perspective of most other developed nations and societies. They know well, the history of slavery in America. They simply can't imagine the remnants of its effect in today's society—why race is still a thing.

While we could see Black Lives Matter posters jouncing up and down in crowds of protesters from Paris to Melbourne and worldwide in the summer of 2020, we know that the movement began at least a decade before those protests. For the most part, those who weren't Black in America couldn't fully understand why it was important to underscore the matter of Black lives. The young people who created the movement were using language—Black Lives Matter—to protest what was hard for others to see and difficult to put their finger on— Calling a thing, a thing.

This language, meant to enlighten and foster understanding of the Black experience, has shifted into political gadgetry in an attempt to discredit and diminish its effectiveness. But it still holds its power.

Language. It is so powerful that it can forge an entire nation through a constitution created to govern a land of diverse people, and it can equally dismantle entire structures of oppression. Language is ammunition. So, it's no wonder today when these young people shout from the rooftops, "We matter!" it enters the ear, mind, and heart of those who care; it germinates and begs the question, why?'

When language is powerful enough, it's impossible for one to remain the same. I'm positive that anyone who demonstrates or becomes an ally for the justice, edification, inclusion, and celebration of Black people, probably first heard something that stirred something in them, and they were never again the same.

Have You Heard Something that Has Stirred You to Ask Why?

The most fundamental purpose for having this type of language is to communicate to others, who we are, the conditions that exist, how it's affected us, their role in it, and how it can be rectified. Black people asking why led to the Fourteenth Amendment, which led to other ratifications. White people asking why led to the Emancipation Proclamation and other cultural advancements. Asking "why" led to freedom.

Despite the libraries full of books, the talks, the protests, we're still explaining in 2023. I'm writing this book to explain it again. At some point, Black people will need to stop explaining why, and others will need to step up and ask for themselves.

Beginning with Why

I can hear some of my dear colleagues now, "But why ask why? You're creating a problem that isn't there. You're pulling the race card on everything, Pepper! It's not about race. If it's not broken, why does it need fixing?"

This is the same biased thought pattern behind the meeting I attended with the financial company executive, recounted at the beginning of Chapter Five, when she asked, "*They* speak English, don't *they?*" In essence, she asked why there was a need to create targeted campaigns for their (revenue-generating) multicultural customers. If the multicultural customer speaks English, just like their white customers, there's no need for what is considered "special treatment." I translated her question to mean: *Why are we asking why?* For her and many, nothing is broken, and nothing needs fixing. However, this attitude derives from the lens and perspective of privilege; it's a strong symptom of blindness or a telling indicator that blind spots are present and preventing them from seeing the reality of others.

From the Black lens, there are definitely some things—*many* things—that are broken. The murder of George Floyd is the strongest, most recent, and most heartbreaking demonstration in modern history of how broken things are.

Have You Listened to Black People Explain What's Broken from Their Eyes?

I've recently begun actively removing the phrase "it goes without saying" from my conversations and even my thinking because if nothing else is clear, there is a disconnect. That's what this entire blind spot conversation is about, disconnects.

Let me explain what I mean . . .

I have been, for decades, sitting in my Black experience, thinking my Black experience is obvious and casually but generally explaining my Black experience to my clients as if they know the nuances of what makes my Black experience unique. I understood that so much more detail was needed for them to *"get it."* Likewise, my white colleagues and clients sit in their white experience, thinking their white experience is obvious—and attainable by anyone who tries hard enough—casually explaining how I, too, can enjoy all of the same privileges they take for granted, if I just pull myself up by the bootstraps. And for them, too, so much more comprehension and compassion on the Black condition is needed for them to *get it.* To "get" that there are no boots big enough or bootstraps strong enough to pull me up—or any other Black person in America, surrounded in the quicksand of racial injustice. Centuries of false promises. Decades of letdowns. Yes, we've made progress. Yes, we're more economically and educationally advanced today than we were one hundred years ago. That does not mean things aren't broken.

As for the subject at hand—how business leaders can understand the history, see the value, then connect with and serve Black consumers—I had a lightbulb moment. I began to devise a new presentation that leaves no stone unturned. In addition to my qualitative research services, I created a deck of insights that break the Black experience all the way down. The Black Insights presentation, my most requested presentation, is a walk through almost everything decision-makers need to know: the fundamentals of Black identity, beliefs, and behaviors, key values, unconscious biases, Black culture redefined, how each generation approached the fight toward equality, and examples of brands that are striving to get it right. I engage my clients and refrain from finger-pointing; nevertheless, I tell the truth. It's important to get into those uncomfortable truths because the disconnect seems to lie somewhere between the sincere experiences we've had as individuals, and as a group, and the belief that all of our experiences are the same. They're not.

I hope that you have started to grasp that our differences are important. Sameness is exasperating. Not only do we look different, we think differently. We act differently. We believe different things. We behave and speak differently. There are certainly many similarities. But those differences are the very essence of who we are. The differences aren't things to ignore, in an attempt to not feel awkward or believe that you're making us feel awkward. The differences are things to acknowledge and engage.

Have You Asked Yourself Why Differences Are Taboo?

Just as most humans have evolved from being fiercely tribal to crossing continents and joining with other communities and cultures, I'm suggesting an evolution in your thinking about Black people—in your assessment of our value and what equal footing means. To be clear, I'm not asking for anyone's approval or validation of the Black experience. A brilliant quote from the late pioneering actress, entertainer, and activist Diahann Carroll is, "Being Black is not a problem for a Black person. Being Black is a problem for the community that doesn't understand that you are a human being." That is to say that Black people are comfortable in their Blackness. It is revered amongst us—celebrated, humored upon, beloved and sacred. It is why being Black comes with no apologies. That's the meaning of "unapologetically Black."

Instead, I'm asking for an evaluation and evolution of how *you* perceive Black. I'm asking you to ask yourself why Black is, consciously or unconsciously, generally less valuable. Why there's a profound lack of consideration for Black talent and leadership at the table—at your table? Why a particular strategy unquestionably involves a stereotypical placement of a Black mother or father in a particular campaign? Why it's hard to hear that a joke or comment was racially offensive? Why there is widespread divestment in Black consumer targets.

Why? Then What?

Of the manifold answers to these very big questions, *then what*? What could possibly go wrong—or better, go right—in breaking away from "the way it's always been" to a new way of being? More unity? An entire population can express their own cultural uniqueness without being ostracized? Better relationships? More inclusion? Then what: More growth and development? Better bottom lines?

If you're asking these questions and care about the answers, "then what" is a pathway to becoming an ally. I believe we have the opportunity to recalibrate how we operate in this industry and in this country, tap into our intellectual curiosity and create something groundbreaking, positive, and inclusive.

Why Ask Why?

As mentioned throughout this book, the game-changing benefits of asking why can lead to:

- A comprehensive and decision-influencing perspective.
- The formation of real relationships based on confidence, not fear.
- Respect for and celebration of differences.
- Less bias, thus closing the racial and cultural gap.
- Inspiration to create new ways of living, seeing the world, and doing business.

When a leader asks why, perhaps their followers will ask why. When the leader becomes an ally, perhaps their teams will, too. How does one not only say things should be different, but actually become a catalyst for change? What does it mean to be an ally?

26

The Value of Allyship

"Privilege is having a brighter light. Allyship is shining that light in the darkness."

—A. Krause, UBP, Inc.

Maybe you have heard many of the concepts, observations and insights presented in this book in some form or another. Perhaps you've said, "I didn't know!" at some point while reading these chapters, like so many of my clients mentioned throughout this book. Maybe you've even asked yourself, "Why?"

In a nutshell, the goal of this book is three-fold: First, I reframed the Black experience and put Black in context to demonstrate the relationship between our history and our beliefs and behaviors. Next, I challenged white America and others to confront their biases about Black America and how blind spots can really cause harm. And finally, armed with insights, history, and relief from biases, I want to talk about how to align everything you've learned for your leading role as an ally.

We don't just build community—we cultivate it through conversation. Let your internal dialogue always have a place in your life as external dialogue because that's where change and growth occur. —Ally Love

A great start is a series of conversations. When guiding my clients through bridge-building workshops, I suggest having a set of conversation-starters and questions that allow for honest dialogue.

Where is your internal dialogue guiding you? What have been the outcomes of a conversation with your team? It's possible to have a laser-focused single talk. But from my experience, this allyship business will likely be a journey. When allies commit to the journey, the results are much more promising and long-lasting than a quick five-point-agenda meeting. Not always, but most times, hurried chats result in policies, decisions, and campaigns that miss the mark, fail to resonate, and don't last. Allyship is a marathon, not a sprint. We see that the way "it's always been done" has, for a long time, rejected what could have been meaningful connections. Exclusionary and outdated thinking has created a wide and deep chasm for us all. But our generation can be the ones who lessen that chasm. As time goes on and deeper understanding occurs, something in your reasoning, something in this language, will begin to challenge your norm, hinting about a better, more cooperative way of doing things.

Let's start with the following four Black Affirmations. An ally believes:

1. Black people are valuable—*period.*

Black consumers have tremendous spending power in the market-place, it's true. But that's not the value I speak of; it's broader. Removing the consumer aspect for a second, Black people matter. They have intrinsic value. They hold cultural stock. They are profoundly optimistic and loyal. As consumers, they're worth understanding, including and celebrating.

2. Black people are safe.

Black people are not inherently dangerous. They are altruistic, friendly, good-natured, and have the biggest hearts for forgiveness. They are gatekeepers who rightfully protect all that they deem important.

3. Black people are desirable.

Black people are beautiful, attractive and desirable. They are accept-able in all of the unique ways that make them different, and these differences are not deficiencies or aspects of their culture that need to be fixed. They are included and celebrated for their skin shades, their hair texture, their body composition, their facial features and their choice of expression. Not only in the physical, but the non-physical as well. They are articulate, funny, helpful and reliable.

4. Black people are capable.

Black people are able to do any and every thing they desire. They are limitless. They are inclusive. They're educated, enterprising, creative and original. They are resilient, wise and prudent. Black people are capable.

As one reads this list, it's possible that it won't be readily accepted. There may be knee-jerk rebuttals to any or all of the truths above. Here is the perfect opportunity to dig into *why* that is. Dig up all of the beliefs you may hold, about the Black affirmations above. Ask why. Further, probe to find out how those beliefs have benefited you thus far, and what you can do to eradicate those biases. Use the Seven Blind Spots to reaffirm the insights you've learned in Part Two, Chapters 3–9.

If you do in fact believe the Black affirmations above, how do these beliefs align with your policies and strategies—both historically and for the future? If you believe that Black is valuable, Black is safe, Black is desirable and Black is capable, but you *aren't* representing Black in a way that affirms your beliefs, it's time to find out why—and then take action to get those two aspects aligned. Your beliefs as an ally must be reflected in your decisions and how you approve what's new and next in your company, for your brand and regarding your policies.

Let's take Affirmation #2 and Affirmation #3, for example. As an ally, you believe Black consumers are safe and desirable. If you operate a travel company, such as an airline or hotel brand, is there an accurate and acceptable amount of representation in your company? The same could be asked about how Black representation ranks in campaigns and messaging. Do you believe that placing a happy Black family on the beach, enjoying a holiday away, resonates with your idea of a safe, desirable and carefree vacation?

It Is Time To Tell a New Story.

In addition to my "core four" Black Affirmations, what are your affirming beliefs about Black consumers? It may be easier to start with Black people you know—perhaps a friend, neighbor, or family member. What do you know for sure about them? Add those things to your personal Black Affirmations list, and let it grow!

Other Black Ally Attributes
Familiar

Familiar has its roots in the word 'family' and has a similar meaning. Not only is it important to be familiar with issues that affect Black consumers on micro and macro levels, but it's also important to have representation on your team—people who understand the language and nuances that speak to the Black experience. How do you feel connected and involved with your Black customers in ways that you would be with a family member?

Take Ben & Jerry's ice cream, for example. If they maintained ice cream making and never made a cultural or political statement, most of their Black consumer base would likely keep buying their ice cream. However, it seemed necessary in their pursuit to be an ally, to speak up. They launched an awareness campaign titled "Silence is NOT an Option." In 2020 and 2021, they decided to get involved with what was happening with their customers affected by compounding racial tension. Further, they created a dedicated flavor, "Pecan Resist," to lend their hand in the protest and policies toward change. A limited-edition flavor made by the company, "Change is Brewing" was designed to support Congresswoman Cori Bush, author and Missouri State Representative who introduced a public safety bill, the People's Response Act, calling for states to reallocate resources towards community-driven safety and protection, rather than solely carceral-driven safety and protection by traditional law enforcement.

Investors

We discussed the importance of investing in Black Media in Chapter 19, and the characteristics of a winning brand in Part Five. One-offs won't get the job done; neither will we, by merely talk about solutions. We need action. Investment-in-action—like that demonstrated by P&G's chief brand officer, Marc Pritchard—consistently promotes how Black leadership and representation matter. Are you investing in Black research? Are there Black managers, directors, leaders, and consultants who make up part of the whole team? Have you thought about employing a plan of action, like Pixar (Chapter 24), and building cultural trust? These types of investments cannot only directly impact how decisions and strategies concerning Black consumers are carried out. Investing in Black involvement to create strategies and launch kick-ass campaigns benefits everyone. Remember Black Affirmation #4—Black people are capable and inclusive.

Equitable

Equality means each individual or group of people is given the same resources or opportunities. Equity recognizes that each person has different circumstances and allocates the resources and opportunities needed to achieve an equal outcome. Both are important. However, an ally's equity position is the key to delivering outstanding support and an evolved approach toward addressing consumer needs and challenges.

As an ally, to get your plan of action in place, we need a plan, and we need follow-through. Ask: What is the initiative? When does it start, and when does it end? Whom does it involve; who is needed to make it work? What are the metrics of impact? Getting specific—better yet, implementing an "ally trust" team dedicated to the details and duration of the initiative gets things off the ground. It starts with a decision to *want* to do it and then to try. And maybe getting it right involves trying and trying again—That's fine! Diversitydreaming.com thinks of being an ally like this:

take   **A**CTION
LIVE honestly
LIFT others
YOU can make a difference

○   ✖

Making the PAK

Being an ally could mean structural changes in your organization. Model it from the top down and implement policies that make a difference with periodic oversight. Make the PAK:

Put Your Money Where Your Target Is: Invest in Black market research, Black media, and Black human capital.

Accountability: Create internal and external messaging that declares the company's mission, promise statements, and actions.

Keep Your Promises: Whatever you do, don't go back on promises to your Black consumer target.

What happens when leaders become allies with Black consumers? It could lead to a highly profitable impact and change lives. It **doesn't** mean that anyone has to fear losing out or that Black people will take their places somehow—quite the contrary. Allyship works to guarantee a better outcome for everyone. It means equitable opportunities, inclusive workplace practices, an improved market research industry, and ultimately, happier consumers—*a better bottom line!*

The involvement necessary to truly be an ally does not have to be labor intensive. Still, it may take some internal and systemic rearranging (which, in turn, can make some uncomfortable). The results are worth it, however. And when the right kind of investments are made, especially educational investments (learning and embracing Black American history), maybe even *you* will be able to "explain Black" in the way that I do, in a way that helps your company and the country see that Black is valuable.

Acknowledgments

I am grateful for my Sisterhood and Brotherhood who supported this journey

You have been by my truth-tellers who root for me, no matter what. Thanks for the encouragement, your ears and shoulders of support, for providing honest feedback, and for showing up again and again and again.

Sisterhood

Jo Jackson, Marti Worell, Joan Sanders, Deborah Robinson Flemister, Celina Farquhar, Amy Hilliard, Beverly Hunter, Gwen Downing, Leana Flowers, Lauren Elle Prather, Kay Humphries, Pam Smith, BJ Parker, Carla Burgess, Bridget Howard, Linda Ruffins, Marion Batey, Pattie Cantella, Peggy Mullins

Brotherhood

David Luckett, Ron Miller, Mark Polsfuss, Mark Guerrero, Brad Sanders, Mike Ferguson, Pete Bermudez, Victor James, Sr., Joseph Randall, Micheal L. Peery, Greg Wilson

Coaches that make the path clear

Karyn Pettigrew

R. Sporty King

Publisher: Paramount Market Publishing, Inc.

Doris Walsh and **Jim Madden:** Thank you for encouraging me to begin the book-writing journey. Three books later, here we are. Thank you for getting "it." Thank you for your confidence, instinct, and insight. Thank you for being so patient. Thank you for your unwavering support. **Anne Kilgore:** You were brilliant at pulling the manuscript together and making the pages look good. Thank you!

Special Thanks for your time, thoughtful conversations, and insights

Reverend Doctor Otis Moss, III, Reverend Kevin Murphy, Autumn McDonald, Ivan Burwell, Dr. Edward Rincon, Don Moore, Dee Dixon, Alfred Edmond, Jr., Deborah Gray Young, Reginald Osborne, Detavio Samuels, Dr. Hermene Hartman, Professor Ariela Nerubay Turndorf, Ty Johnson, Melody McDowell, Twyler Jenkins, Brenda Lee, Ray Celaya, Professor Yla Eason, Nia Hall

I am grateful to all the Business Leaders who invest in Black American market research studies and the respondents who participate.

Index

245

About the Authors

PEPPER MILLER
President, Hunter Miller Group

Pepper Miller is a recognized researcher, author, thought leader, and Black American subject matter expert.

She founded The Hunter-Miller Group (HMG) in 1995, a Chicago-based, leading-edge market research and strategic planning firm. Since then, Pepper has been helping Fortune 500 companies and non-profits better understand and positively engage Black America to have loyal customers and a positive bottom line.

Some of these clients include AARP, Bravo, CNN, McDonald's, Procter&Gamble, Unilever, Walgreens, U.S. Bank, The Chicago Symphony Orchestra, and more.

Before writing this book, Pepper co-authored with the late Herb Kemp, *What's Black About It?* and authored *Black STILL Matters in Marketing.* Both books are considered the most important references to Black consumer insights by many business leaders in the marketing industry.

Pepper is able to help audiences think differently about Black America and dig deeper into the Black American psyche by talking about both simple ideas and taboo topics.

It's this ability that earned Pepper several awards, including The Insights Association Laureate Recognition (2021), ICABA Women of Impact (2022), MOBE Spirit of D. Park Gibson Award for Excellence in Market Research (2018), Target Market News' MAAX Award for Market Research Executive of the Year (2007) and MAFA Trailblazer Award (2014).

Pepper is an Executive Sponsor to OverIndex, a community of Black Market Researchers and Strategists to provide research and strategy opportunities and encourage the market research industry to be more inclusive so that **Who** is doing the research and **How** research is being done become relevant approaches within the industry.

Pepper is also a founding blogger for *Advertising Age's Big Tent* multicultural blog, has blogged for *Forbes* and *The Medium,* and enjoys engaging with and mentoring young professionals.

Victoria Lynn Childress

Victoria Lynn Childress has been an entrepreneur, writer, and creative consultant at her
agency for nearly twenty years. She writes non-fiction for authors and
marketing copy for corporate clients. As a writer and communications
consultant, she has produced award-winning campaigns and best-selling
books. Her father was the first Black student to attend a desegregated
high school in the south, and that history, along with living in the racially
historic city of Memphis, sparked a light of Black consciousness, light,
and clarity she carries into her work. She is passionate about all things
Black and finds meaning in projects that express the history and future
of Black people in America.

She attended college in Rome and later immigrated to Italy from
the United States, where she now lives. Victoria raises her Daughter and
leads a summer abroad exchange, international college tour, and writing
program, primarily for Black teenage girls and girls of color. Just as she
teaches and creates travel-based educational experiences for her own
Daughter, she hopes that through travel, her students can explore the
many options and opportunities available to them for college, career,
and life abroad.

For more information on purchasing additional copies of this
book contact Paramount Market Publishing at 607-275-8100.